NUMBER THE STARS

LOIS LOWRY

WORKBOOK

Contents

'아동 도서계의 노벨상!' 미국 최고 권위의 아동 문학상

뉴베리 상(Newbery Award)은 미국 도서관 협회에서 해마다 미국 아동 문학 발전에 가장 크게 이바지한 작가에게 수여하는 아동 문학상입니다. 1922년에 시작된 이 상은 미국에서 가장 오래 역사를 지닌 아동 문학상이자, '아동 도서계의 노벨상'이라 불릴 만큼 높은 권위를 자랑하는 상입니다.

뉴베리 상은 그 역사와 권위만큼이나 심사 기준이 까다롭기로 유명한데, 심사단은 책의 주제 의식은 물론 정보의 깊이와 스토리의 정교함, 캐릭터와 문체의 적정성 등을 꼼꼼히 평가하여 수상작을 결정합니다.

그해 최고의 작품으로 선정된 도서에게는 '뉴베리 메달(Newbery Medal)'이라고 부르는 금색 메달을 수여하며, 최종 후보에 올랐던 주목할 만한 작품들에게는 '뉴베리 아너(Newbery Honor)'라는 이름의 은색 마크를 수여합니다.

뉴베리 상을 받은 도서는 미국의 모든 도서관에 비치되어 더 많은 독자들을 만나게 되며, 대부분 수십에서 수백만 부가 판매되는 베스트셀러가 됩니다. 뉴베리 상을 수상한 작가는 그만큼 필력과 작품성을 인정받게 되어, 수상 작가의 다른 작품들 또한 수상작 못지않게 커다란 주목과 사랑을 받습니다.

왜 뉴베리 수상작인가?
쉬운 어휘로 쓰인 '검증된' 영어원서!

뉴베리 수상작들은 '검증된 원서'로 국내 영어 학습자들에게 큰 사랑을 받고 있습니다. 뉴베리 수상작이 원서 읽기에 좋은 교재인 이유는 무엇일까요?

1. 아동 문학인 만큼 어휘가 어렵지 않습니다.
2. 어렵지 않은 어휘를 사용하면서도 '문학상'을 수상한 만큼 문장의 깊이가 상당합니다.
3. 적당한 난이도의 어휘와 깊이 있는 문장으로 구성되어 있기 때문에 초등 고학년부터 성인까지, 영어 초보자부터 실력자까지 모든 영어 학습자들이 읽기에 좋습니다.

실제로 뉴베리 수상작은 국제중·특목고에서는 입시 필독서로, 대학교에서는 영어 강독 교재로 다양하고 폭넓게 활용되고 있습니다. 이런 이유로 뉴베리 수상작은 한국어 번역서보다 오히려 원서가 훨씬 많이 판매되는 기현상을 보이고 있습니다.

'베스트 오브 베스트'만을 엄선한「뉴베리 컬렉션」

「뉴베리 컬렉션」은 뉴베리 메달 및 아너 수상작, 그리고 뉴베리 수상 작가의 유명 작품들을 엄선하여 한국 영어 학습자들을 위한 최적의 교재로 재탄생시킨 영어 원서 시리즈입니다.

1. 어휘 수준과 문장의 난이도, 분량 등 국내 영어 학습자들에게 적합한 정도를 종합적으로 검토하여 선정하였습니다.
2. 기존 원서 독자층 사이의 인기도까지 감안하여 최적의 작품들을 선별하였습니다.
3. 판형이 좁고 글씨가 작아 읽기 힘들었던 원서 디자인을 대폭 수정하여, 판형을 시원하게 키우고 읽기에 최적화된 영문 서체를 사용하여 가독성을 극대화하였습니다.
4. 함께 제공되는 워크북은 어려운 어휘를 완벽하게 정리하고 이해력을 점검하는 퀴즈를 덧붙여 독자들이 원서를 보다 쉽고 재미있게 읽을 수 있도록 구성하였습니다.
5. 기존에 높은 가격에 판매되어 구입이 부담스러웠던 오디오북을 부록으로 제공하여 리스닝과 소리 내어 읽기에까지 원서를 두루 활용할 수 있도록 했습니다.

로이스 로리(Lois Lowry)는 1937년 하와이 호놀룰루에서 태어난 미국의 청소년 문학 작가입니다. 언니의 죽음을 자전적으로 다룬 첫 소설「그 여름의 끝(A Summer to Die)」으로 단숨에 독자들을 사로잡은 그녀는, 2차 세계대전을 배경으로 인간의 존엄성과 가치를 되새기게 하는 문제작「별을 헤아리며(Number the Stars)」로 1990년 첫 번째 뉴베리 메달을 수상했습니다. 이어 1994년에는 인간의 어두운 면을 파헤치며 미래 사회에 대한 질문을 던진 수작「기억 전달자(The Giver)」로 다시 뉴베리 메달을 수상했는데, 한 작가가 뉴베리 아너도 아닌 메달을 두 번이나 수상한 것은 극히 이례적인 일로 그녀의 뛰어난 작품성을 확인할 수 있는 단적인 예라고 할 수 있습니다.

「Number the Stars」는 유태인 추방 및 학살이 일어나고 있는 나치 통치하의 덴마크를 배경으로 10살 소녀 안네마리와 가족들이 유대인 친구 엘렌을 숨겨 주면서 벌어지는 일을 잔잔하면서도 긴박감 있게 담아낸 소설입니다. 제목「Number the Stars」는 성경의 시편 147편 "그가 별들의 수를 헤아리시고 그들 모두 그 이름대로 부르시는도다"에서 가지고 온 것으로, 여기서 별은 '다윗의 별' 즉 유태인을 상징하는 동시에, '하나님의 온 우주의 별을 모두 헤아리고 이름을 불러주듯 세상에 의미 없는 존재는 없다'라는 의미를 함축적으로 담아내며 '인간의 존엄성'에 대해서 한번 더 생각해보도록 합니다.

「Number the Stars」는「별을 헤아리며」라는 제목으로 번역되었는데 원서의 영어 수준이 어렵지 않아 오히려 번역서보다 원서가 더 많이 판매되는 기현상이 벌어지는 책 중 하나입니다. 일반적으로는 로이스 로리의 다른 작품「The Giver」가 더 유명하지만, 원서를 많이 읽은 마니아들 사이에선 감동과 재미, 쉬운 영어 수준 등 모든 면에서「Number the Stars」가 더 높은 평가를 받고 있습니다.

원서 본문

내용이 담긴 원서 본문입니다.

원어민이 읽는 일반 원서와 같은 텍스트지만, 암기해야 할 중요 어휘들은 볼드체로 표시되어 있습니다. 이 어휘들은 지금 들고 계신 워크북에 챕터별로 정리되어 있습니다.

학습 심리학 연구 결과에 따르면, 한 단어씩 따로 외우는 단어 암기는 거의 효과가 없다고 합니다. 단어를 제대로 외우기 위해서는 문맥(Context) 속에서 단어를 암기해야 하며, 한 단어당 문맥 속에서 15번 이상 마주칠 때 완벽하게 암기할 수 있다고 합니다.

이 책의 본문에서는 중요 어휘를 볼드체로 강조하여, 문맥 속의 단어들을 더 확실히 인지(Word Cognition in Context)하도록 돕고 있습니다. 또한 대부분의 중요 단어들은 다른 챕터에서도 반복해서 등장하기 때문에 이 책을 읽는 것만으로도 자연스럽게 어휘력을 향상시킬 수 있습니다.

또한 본문 하단에는 내용 이해를 돕기 위한 '각주'가 첨가되어 있습니다. 각주는 굳이 암기할 필요는 없지만, 알아 두면 도움이 될 만한 정보를 설명하고 있습니다. 각주를 참고하면 스토리를 더 깊이 있게 이해할 수 있어 원서를 읽는 재미가 배가됩니다.

워크북(Workbook)

Check Your Reading Speed

해당 챕터의 단어 수가 기록되어 있어, 리딩 속도를 측정할 수 있습니다. 특히 리딩 속도를 중시하는 독자들이 유용하게 사용할 수 있습니다.

Build Your Vocabulary

본문에 볼드 표시되어 있던 단어들이 정리되어 있습니다. 리딩 전·후에 반복해서 보면 원서를 더욱 쉽게 읽을 수 있고, 어휘력도 빠르게 향상될 것입니다.

단어는 〈스펠링 - 빈도 - 발음기호 - 품사 - 한글 뜻 - 영문 뜻〉 순서로 표기되어 있으며 빈도 표시(★)가 많을수록 필수 어휘입니다. 반복해서 등장하는 단어는 빈도 대신 '복습'으로 표기되어 있습니다. 품사는 아래와 같이 표기했습니다.

n. 명사 │ a. 형용사 │ ad. 부사 │ vi. 자동사 │ vt. 타동사 │ v. 자·타동사 모두 쓰이는 동사

conj. 접속사 │ prep. 전치사 │ int. 감탄사 │ phrasal v. 구동사 │ idiom 숙어 및 관용구

Comprehension Quiz

간단한 퀴즈를 통해 읽은 내용에 대한 이해력을 점검해 볼 수 있습니다.

「뉴베리 컬렉션」 이렇게 읽어 보세요!

아래와 같이 프리뷰(Preview) → 리딩(Reading) → 리뷰(Review) 세 단계를 거치면서 읽으면, 더욱 효과적으로 영어 실력을 향상할 수 있습니다.

1. 프리뷰(Preview) : 오늘 읽을 내용을 먼저 점검하자!

• 워크북을 통해 오늘 읽을 챕터에 나와 있는 단어들을 쭉 훑어봅니다. 어떤 단어들이 나오는지, 내가 아는 단어와 모르는 단어는 어떤 것들이 있는지 가벼운 마음으로 살펴봅니다.

• 평소처럼 하나하나 쓰면서 암기하려고 하지는 마세요! 익숙하지 않은 단어들을 주의 깊게 보되, 어차피 리딩을 하면서 점차 익숙해질 단어라는 것을 기억하며 빠르게 훑어봅니다.

• 뒤 챕터로 갈수록 '복습'이라고 표시된 단어들이 늘어나는 것을 알 수 있습니다. '복습' 단어인데도 여전히 익숙하지 않다면 더욱 신경을 써서 봐야겠죠? 매일매일 꾸준히 읽는다면, 익숙한 단어들이 점점 많아진다는 것을 몸으로 느낄 수 있습니다.

2. 리딩(Reading) : 내용에 집중하며 빠르게 읽어 나가자!

• 프리뷰를 마친 후 바로 리딩을 시작합니다. 방금 살펴봤던 어휘들을 문장 속에서 다시 만나게 되는데, 이 과정에서 단어의 쓰임새와 어감을 자연스럽게 익히게 됩니다.

• 모르는 단어나 이해되지 않는 문장이 나오더라도 멈추지 말고 전체적인 맥락을 파악하면서 속도감 있게 읽어 나가세요. 이해되지 않는 문장들은 따로 표시를 하되, 일단 넘어가고 계속 읽는 것이 좋습니다. 뒷부분을 읽다 보면 자연히 이해가 되는 경우도 있고, 정 이해가 되지 않는 부분은 리딩을 마친 이후에 따로 리뷰하는 시간을 가지면 됩니다. 문제집을 풀듯이 모든 문장을 분석하면서 원서를 읽는 것이 아니라, 리딩을 할 때는 리딩에만, 리뷰를 할 때는 리뷰에만 집중하는 것이 필요합니다.

• 볼드 처리된 단어의 의미가 궁금하더라도 워크북을 바로 펼치지 마세요. 정 궁금하다면 한 번씩 참고하는 것도 나쁘진 않지만, 워크북과 원서를 번갈아 보면서 읽는 것은 리딩의 흐름을 끊고 단어 하나하나에 집착하는 좋지 않은 리딩 습관을 심어 줄 수 있습니다.

• 같은 맥락에서 번역서를 구해 원서와 동시에 번갈아 보는 것도 좋은 방법이 아닙니다. 한글 번역을 가지고 있다고 해도 일단 영어로 읽을 때는 영어에만 집중하고 어느 정도 분량을 읽은 후에 번역서와 비교하도록 하세요. 모든 문장을

일일이 번역해서 완벽하게 이해하려는 것은 오히려 좋지 않은 리딩 습관을 심어 주어 장기적으로는 바람직하지 않은 결과를 얻을 수 있습니다. 처음부터 완벽하게 이해하려고 하는 것보다는 빠른 속도로 2~3회 반복해서 읽는 방식이 실력 향상에 더 도움이 됩니다. 만일 반복해서 읽어도 내용이 전혀 이해되지 않아 곤란하다면 책 선정에 문제가 있다고 할 수 있습니다. 그럴 때는 좀 더 쉬운 책을 골라 실력을 다진 뒤 다시 도전하는 것이 좋습니다.

• 초보자라면 분당 150단어의 리딩 속도를 목표로 잡고 리딩을 합니다. 분당 150단어는 원어민이 말하는 속도로, 영어 학습자들이 리스닝과 스피킹으로 넘어가기 위해 가장 기초적으로 달성해야 하는 단계입니다. 분당 50~80단어 정도의 낮은 리딩 속도를 가지고 있는 경우는 대부분 영어 실력이 부족해서라기보다 '잘못된 리딩 습관'을 가지고 있어서 그렇습니다. 이해력이 조금 떨어진다고 하더라도 분당 150단어까지는 속도에 대한 긴장감을 놓치지 말고 속도감 있게 읽어 나가도록 하세요.

3. 리뷰(Review) : 이해력을 점검하고 꼼꼼하게 다시 살펴보자!

• 해당 챕터의 Comprehension Quiz를 통해 이해력을 점검해 봅니다.
• 오늘 만난 어휘들을 다시 한번 복습합니다. 이때는 읽으면서 중요하다고 생각했던 단어를 연습장에 써 보면서 꼼꼼하게 외우는 것도 좋습니다.
• 이해가 되지 않는다고 표시해 두었던 부분도 주의 깊게 분석해 봅니다. 다시 한번 문장을 꼼꼼히 읽고, 어떤 이유에서 이해가 되지 않았는지 생각해 봅니다. 따로 메모를 남기거나 노트를 작성하는 것도 좋은 방법입니다.
• 사실 꼼꼼히 리뷰하는 것은 매우 고된 과정입니다. 원서를 읽고 리뷰하는 시간을 가지는 것이 영어 실력 향상에 많은 도움이 되기는 하지만, 이 과정을 철저히 지키려다가 원서 읽기의 재미를 반감시키는 것은 바람직하지 않습니다. 그럴 때는 차라리 리뷰를 가볍게 하는 것이 좋을 수 있습니다. '내용에 빠져서 재미있게', 문제집에서는 상상도 못할 '많은 양'을 읽으면서, 매일매일 조금씩 꾸준히 실력을 키워 가는 것이 원서를 활용하는 기본적인 방법이며, 영어 공부의 왕도입니다. 문제집 풀듯이 원서 읽기를 시도하고 접근해서는 실패할 수밖에 없습니다.
• 이런 방식으로 원서를 끝까지 다 읽었다면, 다시 반복해서 읽거나 오디오북을 활용하는 등 다양한 방식으로 원서 읽기를 확장해 나갈 수 있습니다. 이에 대한 자세한 안내가 워크북 말미에 실려 있습니다.

1.
Why Are You Running?

1. Why were Annemarie and Ellen running down the street?

   (A) They were practicing for the athletic meet.
   (B) They were running away from the German police.
   (C) They were playing a war game.
   (D) Ellen wanted to win the girls' race that week.

2. Annemarie stared at the German soldiers' _____ before she looked at their faces.

   (A) helmets
   (B) shiny boots
   (C) uniforms
   (D) rifles

3. The soldiers had been in Copenhagen for _____ years.

   (A) 2
   (B) 3
   (C) 4
   (D) 5

4. Why did Annemarie need to tell Mama about the soldiers?

   (A) Kirsti told Mama about the soldiers first.
   (B) She wanted to make her mother nervous.
   (C) She thought it was important to tell her mother about the soldiers.
   (D) She needed to know a new route to take to school.

5. According to Mama, the German soldiers were edgy because _____.

   (A) the children at Annemarie's school started fights with German police
   (B) school children were running on the streets
   (C) Sweden was bombed by resistance fighters
   (D) Nørrebro and Hillerød were bombed by resistance fighters

6. Which of the following was NOT an example of the Resistance?

   (A) Danish people hid bombs and explosives in Nazi factories.
   (B) Danish people damaged railroads.
   (C) Danish people burned books and newspapers from the library.
   (D) Danish people damaged German soldiers' trucks and cars.

7. Why couldn't Annemarie and Kirsti eat butter or cupcakes?

   (A) Her mother wanted them to be healthy.
   (B) Their family could not afford those kinds of foods.
   (C) Those foods were not available in Copenhagen for at least a year.
   (D) Only the adults were allowed to eat those kinds of foods.

✿ *Check Your Reading Speed*

1분에 몇 단어를 읽는지 리딩 속도를 측정해보세요.

$$\frac{1{,}843 \text{ words}}{\text{reading time ( ) sec}} \times 60 = (\quad) \text{ WPM}$$

✿ *Build Your Vocabulary*

race***
[reis]
① v. 질주하다, 경주하다, 달리다; n. 경주 ② n. 인종, 민족
If you race somewhere, you go there as quickly as possible.

adjust**
[ədʒʌ́st]
v. (옷매무새 등을) 바로 하다; 조절하다, 조정하다; 적응하다
If you adjust something such as your clothing or a machine, you correct or alter its position or setting.

leather***
[léðər]
n. 가죽
Leather is treated animal skin which is used for making shoes, clothes, bags, and furniture.

even***
[íːvən]
a. 평평한, 평탄한, 들쑥날쑥하지 않은; ad. 한층, 더욱; 오히려, 정말로
(evenly ad. 고르게, 평탄하게)
An even surface is smooth and flat.

make a face
idiom 얼굴을 찌푸리다, 침울한 표정을 짓다
If you make a face, you twist your face to indicate a certain mental or emotional state.

beat***
[biːt]
v. 패배시키다, 이기다; 치다, 두드리다; (심장, 맥박 등이) 뛰다; n. [음악] 박자; 고동
If you beat someone in a competition or election, you defeat them.

civilized**
[sívəlàizd]
a. 교양 있는, 품위 있는, 문명화 된
If you describe a person or their behavior as civilized, you mean that they are polite and reasonable.

stocky
[stáki]
a. 땅딸막한, 작고 다부진
A stocky person has a body that is broad, solid, and often short.

lanky
[lǽŋki]
a. 마르고 키 큰, 호리호리한
If you describe someone as lanky, you mean that they are tall and thin and move rather awkwardly.

athletic**
[æθlétik]
a. (운동) 경기의; 체육의; 운동선수용의 (athletic meet n. 운동회)
Athletic means relating to athletes and athletics.

plead**
[pliːd]
v. 간청하다, 탄원하다; 변론하다, 변호하다
If you plead with someone to do something, you ask them in an intense, emotional way to do it.

hesitate**
[hézətèit]
v. 주저하다, 머뭇거리다, 망설이다
If you hesitate, you do not speak or act for a short time, usually because you are uncertain, embarrassed, or worried about what you are going to say or do.

shift**
[ʃift]

v. 옮기다, 방향을 바꾸다; n. 변화, 이동; 교대
If you shift something or if it shifts, it moves slightly.

rucksack
[rʌ́ksæk]

n. (등산용) 배낭
A rucksack is a bag with straps that go over your shoulders, so that you can carry things on your back.

residential*
[rèzidénʃəl]

a. 주거의, 거주하기 좋은, 주택지의
A residential area contains houses rather than offices or factories.

sidewalk**
[sáidwɔ̀:k]

n. (포장한) 보도, 인도
A sidewalk is a path with a hard surface by the side of a road.

silvery*
[sílvəri]

a. 은 같은, 은빛의, 은백색의
Silvery things look like silver or are the color of silver.

pigtail
[pígtèil]

n. 땋아 늘인 머리 (돼지 꼬리와 비슷한 모양에서 유래)
If someone has a pigtail or pigtails, their hair is plaited or braided into one or two lengths.

bounce*
[bauns]

v. 튀(게 하)다; 급히 움직이다, 뛰어다니다; n. 튐, 바운드
If something bounces off a surface or is bounced off it, it reaches the surface and is reflected back.

wail**
[weil]

v. (큰소리로) 투덜거리다; 울부짖다, 통곡하다; n. 울부짖음, 비탄, 한탄
If you wail something, you say it in a loud, high-pitched voice that shows that you are unhappy or in pain.

outdistance
[autdístəns]

vt. 훨씬 앞서다, 능가하다
If you outdistance your opponents in a contest of some kind, you beat them easily.

untie*
[ʌntái]

vt. 풀다, 끄르다; 자유롭게 하다 (united a. 묶이지 않은)
If you untie something such as string or rope, you undo it so that there is no knot or so that it is no longer tying something.

skirt***
[skə:rt]

v. 언저리를 지나다, 비켜가다; 경계[변두리]에 있다; n. 스커트, 치마; 교외, 변두리
If you skirt something, you go around the edge of it.

elderly*
[éldərli]

a. 나이가 지긋한
You use elderly as a polite way of saying that someone is old.

string***
[striŋ]

n. 끈, 줄, 실
String is thin rope made of twisted threads, used for tying things together or tying up parcels.

carriage**
[kǽridʒ]

n. 유모차; 마차; 탈것, 차
A carriage is a small vehicle in which a baby can lie as it is pushed along.

pant**
[pænt]

vi. 헐떡거리다, 숨차다; n. 헐떡거림, 숨 가쁨
If you pant, you breathe quickly and loudly with your mouth open, because you have been doing something energetic.

one's heart skips a beat

idiom (심장이 멎을 정도로) 놀라다, 흥분하다
If your heart skips a beat, you are suddenly shocked or surprised.

stern**
[stɔ́ːrn]

a. 엄한, 단호한
Stern words or actions are very severe.

frighten**
[fráitn]

v. 놀라게 하다, 섬뜩하게 하다; 기겁하다 (frightening a. 무서운)
If something or someone frightens you, they cause you to sudden-ly feel afraid, anxious, or nervous.

plod*
[plɑd]

vi. 터벅터벅 걷다; 꾸준히 일하다
If someone plods they walk slowly and heavily.

pout*
[paut]

n. 입을 삐죽거림, 뿌루퉁한 얼굴; v. 입을 삐죽거리다, 토라지다
If someone is in a pout they stick out their lips, in order to show that they are annoyed.

glare**
[glɛər]

v. 노려보다; 번쩍번쩍 빛나다; n. 섬광; 노려봄
If you glare at someone, you look at them with an angry expression on your face.

plant***
[plænt]

v. 놓다; 심다; 창립하다; n. 식물; 공장, 설비
If you plant something somewhere, you put it there firmly.

block***
[blɑk]

vt. (길 등을) 막다, 방해하다; n. 덩어리, 블록
If you block someone's way, you prevent them from going some-where or entering a place by standing in front of them.

rifle**
[ráifəl]

① n. 라이플총 ② vt. 샅샅이 뒤지다; 강탈하다
A rifle is a gun with a long barrel.

grip
[grip]

v. 꽉 잡다, 움켜잡다; n. 잡음, 움켜쥠; 손잡이
If you grip something, you take hold of it with your hand and contin-ue to hold it firmly.

halt**
[hɔːlt]

v. 멈추다, 정지하다; n. 정지, 휴식, 멈춤
When a person or a vehicle halts or when something halts them, they stop moving in the direction they were going and stand still.

harsh**
[hɑːrʃ]

a. (소리 따위가) 귀에 거슬리는; 거친, 가혹한
Harsh voices and sounds are ones that are rough and unpleasant to listen to.

contempt**
[kəntémpt]

n. 경멸, 모욕
If you have contempt for someone or something, you have no respect for them or think that they are unimportant.

polite**
[pəláit]

a. 예의 바른, 공손한 (politely ad. 예의 바르게)
Someone who is polite has good manners and behaves in a way that is socially correct and not rude to other people.

trail away

phrasal v. (목소리가) 서서히 사라지다 (trail v. 끌다; 뒤쫓다)
If a speaker's voice or a speaker trails away, their voice becomes quieter and they hesitate until they stop speaking completely.

glance***
[glæns]

v. 흘긋 보다, 잠깐 보다; n. 흘긋 봄
If you glance at something or someone, you look at them very quickly and then look away again immediately.

motionless**
[móuʃənlis]

a. 움직이지 않는, 부동의, 정지한
Someone or something that is motionless is not moving at all.

sulk
[sʌlk]

vi. 샐쭉해지다, 부루퉁해지다; n. 샐쭉함, 부루퉁함
If you sulk, you are silent and bad-tempered for a while because you are annoyed about something.

doorway**
[dɔ́:rwèi]

n. 문간, 현관, 출입구
A doorway is a space in a wall where a door opens and closes.

giraffe**
[dʒəræf]

n. [동물] 기린
A giraffe is a large African animal with a very long neck, long legs, and dark patches on its body.

extend***
[iksténd]

v. (손ㆍ발 등을) 뻗다, 늘이다; 넓어지다, 퍼지다
If an object extends from a surface or place, it sticks out from it.

stiff**
[stif]

a. 굳은, 뻣뻣한; 완강한, 완고한
Something that is stiff is firm or does not bend easily.

collar**
[kálər]

n. 칼라, 깃; (개 등의) 목걸이; vt. 깃을 달다
The collar of a shirt or coat is the part which fits round the neck and is usually folded over.

prod
[prad]

v. 찌르다, 쑤시다; 자극하다; n. 찌르기, 찌름
If you prod someone or something, you give them a quick push with your finger or with a pointed object.

tremble*
[trémbəl]

v. 떨다, 떨리다
If you tremble, you shake slightly because you are frightened or cold.

shopkeeper*
[ʃápkì:pər]

n. 가게 주인, 소매상인
A shopkeeper is a person who owns or manages a small shop.

truthful
[trú:θfəl]

a. 진실의, 사실의; 성실한, 정직한 (truthfully ad. 진실하게)
If a person or their comments are truthful, they are honest and do not tell any lies.

sneer*
[sniər]

v. 비웃다, 냉소하다; n. 비웃음, 냉소
If you sneer at someone or something, you express your contempt for them by the expression on your face or by what you say.

rosy-cheeked
[róuzitʃì:kt]

a. 뺨이 불그스레한
rosy (a. 장밋빛의) + cheeked (a. …한 뺨을 가진)

scowl*
[skaul]

vi. 얼굴을 찌푸리다, 싫은 기색을 하다; n. 찌푸린 얼굴
When someone scowls, an angry or hostile expression appears on their face.

stubborn**
[stábərn]

a. 완고한, 고집 센
Someone who is stubborn or who behaves in a stubborn way is determined to do what they want and is very unwilling to change their mind.

defiant*
[difáiənt]

a. 도전적인, 반항적인, 시비조의 (defiantly ad. 도전적으로)
If you say that someone is defiant, you mean they show aggression or independence by refusing to obey someone.

stroke**
[strouk]

① vt. 쓰다듬다, 어루만지다; n. 쓰다듬기, 달램 ② n. 타격, 일격, 치기
If you stroke someone or something, you move your hand slowly and gently over them.

tangle*
[tǽŋgəl]

v. 엉키(게 하)다; n. 엉킴; 혼란 (tangled a. 엉킨, 헝클어진)
If something is tangled or tangles, it becomes twisted together in an untidy way.

obstinate**
[ábstənit]

a. 완고한, 고집 센
If you describe someone as obstinate, you are being critical of them because they are very determined to do what they want, and refuse to change their mind or be persuaded to do something else.

hoodlum
[hú:dləm]

n. (구어) 건달, 깡패
A hoodlum is a violent criminal, especially one who is a member of a group.

resist**
[rizíst]

v. 저항하다, 반대하다, 방해하다
If you resist doing something, or resist the temptation to do it, you stop yourself from doing it although you would like to do it.

scurry*
[skə́:ri]

vi. 종종걸음으로 달리다, 급히 가다
When people or small animals scurry somewhere, they move there quickly and hurriedly, especially because they are frightened.

chatter**
[tʃǽtər]

v. 수다를 떨다, 재잘거리다; 지저귀다
If you chatter, you talk quickly and continuously, usually about things which are not important.

kindergarten*
[kíndərgà:rtn]

n. 유치원
A kindergarten is an informal kind of school for very young children, where they learn things by playing.

landscape**
[lǽndskèip]

n. 풍경, 경치, 조망
The landscape is everything you can see when you look across an area of land, including hills, rivers, buildings, trees, and plants.

lamppost
[lǽmppòust]

n. 가로등의 기둥
lamp (n. 등불) + post (n. 기둥)

trudge*
[trʌdʒ]

v. (지쳐서) 터덜터덜 걷다; n. 터덜터덜 걷기
If you trudge somewhere, you walk there slowly and with heavy steps, especially because you are tired or unhappy.

scold**
[scold]

v. 꾸짖다, 잔소리하다
If you scold someone, you speak angrily to them because they have done something wrong.

description**
[diskrípʃən]

n. 서술, 기술, 묘사
A description of someone or something is an account which explains what they are or what they look like.

poke[*]
[pouk]

v. 찌르다, 쑤시다; n. 찌름, 쑤심
If you poke someone or something, you quickly push them with your finger or with a sharp object.

occupation^{**}
[àkjəpéiʃən]

n. 점령, 점거; 직업, 업무
The occupation of a country happens when it is entered and controlled by a foreign army.

sip^{**}
[sip]

v. 찔끔찔끔 마시다; n. 한 모금
If you sip a drink or sip at it, you drink by taking just a small amount at a time.

flavor^{**}
[fléivər]

vt. 풍미를 더하다, 맛을 내다; n. 풍미, 맛 (flavored a. …의 맛이 나는)
If you flavor food or drink, you add something to it to give it a particular taste.

herb[*]
[həːrb]

n. 허브, 약초, 향료 식물
A herb is a plant whose leaves are used in cooking to add flavor to food, or as a medicine.

anxious^{**}
[ǽŋkʃəs]

a. 걱정하는, 염려하는; 열망하는, 간절히 바라는
(anxiously ad. 걱정스럽게, 불안해하며)
If you are anxious, you are nervous or worried about something.

incident^{**}
[ínsədənt]

n. 일어난 일, 작은 사건
An incident is something that happens, often something that is unpleasant.

humorous^{**}
[hjúːmərəs]

a. 유머러스한, 익살스러운
If someone or something is humorous, they are amusing, especially in a clever or witty way.

uneasy^{**}
[ʌníːzi]

a. 불안한, 걱정되는; 어색한, 불편한
If you are uneasy, you feel anxious, afraid, or embarrassed, because you think that something is wrong or that there is danger.

slap^{**}
[slæp]

v. 찰싹 때리다; 털썩[탁] 놓다; n. 찰싹 (때림)
If you slap someone, you hit them with the palm of your hand.

announce^{***}
[ənáuns]

vt. 알리다, 공고하다, 전하다
If you announce a piece of news or an intention, especially something that people may not like, you say it loudly and clearly, so that everyone you are with can hear it.

reassure[*]
[rìːəʃúər]

vt. 안심시키다
If you reassure someone, you say or do things to make them stop worrying about something.

exaggerate^{**}
[igzǽdʒərèit]

vt. 과장하다
If you exaggerate, you indicate that something is, for example, worse or more important than it really is.

edgy
[édʒi]

a. 초조한; 신랄한
If someone is edgy, they are nervous and anxious, and seem likely to lose control of themselves.

pretend[**]
[priténd]
v. …인 체하다, 가장하다; a. 가짜의, 꾸민
If you pretend that something is the case, you act in a way that is intended to make people believe that it is the case, although in fact it is not.

absorb[**]
[əbsɔ́:r]
vt. 열중시키다; 흡수하다, 빨아들이다 (absorbed a. 열중한, 몰두한)
If something absorbs you, it interests you a great deal and takes up all your attention and energy.

Dane[*]
[dein]
n. 덴마크 사람
A Dane is a person who comes from Denmark.

illegal[**]
[ilí:gəl]
a. 불법의, 비합법적인
If something is illegal, the law says that it is not allowed.

occasional[**]
[əkéiʒənəl]
a. 가끔의, 때때로의 (occasionally ad. 때때로, 가끔)
Occasional means happening sometimes, but not regularly or often.

ordinary[***]
[ɔ́:rdənèri]
a. 보통의, 평범한
Ordinary people or things are normal and not special or different in any way.

sabotage
[sǽbətɑ̀:ʒ]
n. 방해 행위, 파괴 행위, 사보타주; v. 파괴하다; 방해하다
A sabotage is an act to deliberately damage or destroy something in order to hurt.

explode[***]
[iksplóud]
v. 폭발하다, 격발하다; 폭발시키다
If an object such as a bomb explodes or if someone or something explodes it, it bursts loudly and with great force, often causing damage or injury.

industrial[**]
[indʌ́striəl]
a. 산업의, 공업의
You use industrial to describe things which relate to or are used in industry.

transport[**]
[trænspɔ́:rt]
vt. 수송하다, 운반하다; n. 수송기
To transport people or goods somewhere is to take them from one place to another.

overhear[*]
[òuvərhíər]
vt. (overheard–overheard) (상대방 모르게) 우연히 듣다, 엿듣다
If you overhear someone, you hear what they are saying when they are not talking to you and they do not know that you are listening.

determined[*]
[ditə́:rmind]
a. 결연한, 굳게 결심한
If you are determined to do something, you have made a firm decision to do it and will not let anything stop you.

crowd[***]
[kraud]
n. 군중, 인파; v. 군집하다, 붐비다
A crowd is a large group of people who have gathered together, for example to watch or listen to something interesting, or to protest about something.

murmur[*]
[mə́:rmər]
v. 중얼거리다; 투덜거리다; n. 중얼거림
If you murmur something, you say it very quietly, so that not many people can hear what you are saying.

cheek***
[tʃiːk]

n. 뺨, 볼
Your cheeks are the sides of your face below your eyes.

frost**
[frɔːst]

v. (케이크에) 설탕을 입히다; 서리로 덮다, 서리가 앉다; n. 서리
(frosting n. 설탕옷)
If you frost something such as a cake, you give a frost-like surface by putting sugar on it.

impassive
[impǽsiv]

a. 무표정한, 감정이 없는, 무감각한
If someone is impassive or their face is impassive, they are not showing any emotion.

beneath***
[biníːθ]

prep. …의 아래[밑]에, …보다 낮은
Something that is beneath another thing is under the other thing.

2.
Who Is the Man Who Rides Past?

1. All Danish children grew up with _____.

    (A) fairy tales
    (B) seeing Christian X in his palace
    (C) knowing the German guards on the streets
    (D) parties on the streets of Copenhagen

2. Why were the German soldiers in Denmark?

    (A) The Germans fought the Danish people in a fierce battle and the Danish lost.
    (B) The Danish surrendered to the Germans.
    (C) The Germans killed the royal family and took over the country.
    (D) The Germans bombed Demark so Denmark could not fight back.

3. Why didn't the King of Denmark need a bodyguard?

    (A) Any Danish citizen would die to save him.
    (B) The King was a great fighter and he didn't need a bodyguard.
    (C) The King never went outside during the war.
    (D) The German soldiers protected him.

4. Why didn't Denmark defend themselves from Germany?

   (A) The Danish had large mountains so it was difficult to organize an army.
   (B) Too many Danish people would die trying to defend themselves from the German army.
   (C) The King wanted the Germans to protect the Danish people from harm.
   (D) Denmark was a poor country and they didn't have the money to fight Germany.

5. German soldiers were not in _____.

   (A) Holland
   (B) Norway
   (C) Belgium
   (D) Sweden

6. How did Annemarie's sister die?

   (A) She died fighting in the war.
   (B) She died in an accident.
   (C) A German solider shot and killed her on the street.
   (D) She fell off a horse and hit her head.

7. During the war, Peter _____.

   (A) would sing songs and play games with Annemarie and Kirsti
   (B) was always fun loving and happy when he spoke to Annemarie's parents
   (C) would visit the apartment but he would speak quickly to Annemarie's parents
   (D) never visited the Johansens

1분에 몇 단어를 읽는지 리딩 속도를 측정해보세요.

$$\frac{1{,}406 \text{ words}}{\text{reading time (\quad) sec}} \times 60 = (\qquad) \text{ WPM}$$

✿ *Build Your Vocabulary*

beg***
[beg]

vt. 부탁[간청]하다; 구걸하다, 빌다
If you beg someone to do something, you ask them very anxiously or eagerly to do it.

snuggle
[snʌ́gəl]

v. 바싹 파고들다, 달라붙다, 쓸어안다
If you snuggle somewhere, you settle yourself into a warm, comfortable position, especially by moving closer to another person.

fairy tale**
[fɛ́əritèil]

n. 동화, 옛날이야기
A fairy tale is a story for children involving magical events and imaginary creatures.

wrap**
[ræp]

v. (감)싸다; 포장하다; n. 싸개, 덮개
If someone wraps their arms, fingers, or legs around something, they put them firmly around it.

mermaid*
[mɔ́:rmèid]

n. (여자) 인어(人魚)
In fairy stories and legends, a mermaid is a woman with a fish's tail instead of legs, who lives in the sea.

interrupt**
[ìntərʌ́pt]

v. 방해하다, 가로막다, 저지하다
If you interrupt someone who is speaking, you say or do something that causes them to stop.

pretend^{복습}
[priténd]

a. 가짜의, 꾸민; v. …인 체하다, 가장하다
Something that is pretend is not real and exists only in the imagination.

sprinkle**
[spríŋkəl]

vt. (액체·분말 등을) 뿌리다, 끼얹다; 간간이 섞다[포함시키다]; n. 소량, 조금
If you sprinkle a thing with something such as a liquid or powder, you scatter the liquid or powder over it.

ball**
[bɔ:l]

① n. 무도회, 댄스파티 ② n. 공, 공 모양의 것
A ball is a large formal social event at which people dance.

fabulous*
[fǽbjələs]

a. 굉장한, 멋진, 믿어지지 않는
If you describe something as fabulous, you are emphasizing that you like it a lot or think that it is very good.

trim**
[trim]

v. 장식하다; 다듬다, 정돈하다; n. 건물의 외면 장식, 외장; 정돈(된 상태)
If something such as a piece of clothing is trimmed with a type of material or design, it is decorated with it, usually along its edges.

feast **
[fi:st]
n. 축제; 진수성찬; v. 축연을 베풀다; 진수성찬을 먹다
A feast is a large and special meal.

frost 복습
[frɔ:st]
v. (케이크에) 설탕을 입히다; 서리로 덮다, 서리가 앉다; n. 서리
If you frost something such as a cake, you give a frostlike surface by putting sugar on it.

sound asleep
idiom 깊이 잠들어
If someone is sound asleep, they are sleeping very deeply.

murmur 복습
[mə́:rmər]
v. 중얼거리다; 투덜거리다; n. 중얼거림
If you murmur something, you say it very quietly, so that not many people can hear what you are saying.

balcony **
[bǽlkəni]
n. 발코니; (극장의) 2층 특별석
A balcony is a platform on the outside of a building, above ground level, with a wall or railing around it.

subject ***
[sʌ́bdʒikt]
n. 백성, 국민; 주제; 학과; a. 영향을 받는; vt. 복종[종속]시키다
The people who live in or belong to a particular country, usually one ruled by a monarch, are the subjects of that monarch or country.

throne ***
[θroun]
n. 왕좌, 왕위; vi. 왕위에 앉다, 왕권을 쥐다
A throne is a decorative chair used by a king, queen, or emperor on important official occasions.

entertain **
[èntərtéin]
vt. 즐겁게 하다; 대접하다, 환대하다
If a performer, performance, or activity entertains you, it amuses you, interests you, or gives you pleasure.

suitable **
[sú:təbəl]
a. 적당한, 어울리는, 알맞은
Someone or something that is suitable for a particular purpose or occasion is right or acceptable for it.

sidewalk 복습
[sáidwɔ̀:k]
n. (포장한) 보도, 인도
A sidewalk is a path with a hard surface by the side of a road.

pillow **
[pílou]
n. 베개; 머리 받침대
A pillow is a rectangular cushion which you rest your head on when you are in bed.

dim **
[dim]
a. 어둑한, 흐릿한, 희미한; v. 어둑하게 하다, 흐려지다
A dim place is rather dark because there is not much light in it.

solemn **
[sáləm]
a. 엄숙한, 근엄한
Someone or something that is solemn is very serious rather than cheerful or humorous.

surrender **
[səréndər]
v. 항복하다, 내어주다, 넘겨주다; n. 항복, 굴복
If you surrender, you stop fighting or resisting someone and agree that you have been beaten.

errand **
[érənd]
n. 볼일, 용건; 심부름
An errand is a short trip that you make in order to do a job for someone, for example when you go to a shop to buy something for them.

amuse
[əmjúːz]

vt. 즐겁게 하다, 재미나게 하다 (amused a. 즐거워하는)
If something amuses you, it makes you want to laugh or smile.

lap
[læp]

n. 무릎; 한 바퀴; v. 겹치게 하다
If you have something on your lap, it is on top of your legs and near to your body.

shiver
[ʃívər]

v. 전율하다; (추위 · 공포로) 후들후들 떨다; n. 떨림, 전율
When you shiver, your body shakes slightly because you are cold or frightened.

consider
[kənsídər]

v. 고려하다, 숙고하다
If you consider something, you think about it carefully.

crochet
[krouʃéi]

v. 코바늘로 뜨개질하다; v. 코바늘 뜨개질
If you crochet, you make cloth by using a needle with a small hook at the end.

lacy
[léisi]

a. 레이스의, 레이스 같은
Lacy things are made from lace or have pieces of lace attached to them.

edging
[édʒiŋ]

n. 가장자리 장식, 테 두름
Edging is something that is put along the borders or sides of something else, usually to make it look attractive.

trousseau
[trúːsou]

n. 혼수 옷가지, 혼숫감
A trousseau is a collection of clothes and other possessions that a bride brings with her when she gets married.

thread
[θred]

n. 실, 바느질 실; vt. 실을 꿰다
A thread is a long very thin piece of a material such as cotton, nylon, or silk, especially one that is used in sewing.

intricate
[íntrəkit]

a. 뒤얽힌, 복잡한
You use intricate to describe something that has many small parts or details.

border
[bɔ́ːrdər]

n. 테두리, 가장자리; 경계; v. 접경하다, 인접하다; 테를 두르다
A border is a strip or band around the edge of something.

enormous
[inɔ́ːrməs]

a. 엄청난, 거대한, 막대한
You can use enormous to emphasize the great degree or extent of something.

fierce
[fiərs]

a. 격렬한, 지독한; 사나운 (fiercely ad. 맹렬하게)
Fierce conditions are very intense, great, or strong.

crush
[krʌʃ]

v. 으스러뜨리다, 짓밟다, 눌러 부수다
To crush a protest or movement, or a group of opponents, means to defeat it completely, usually by force.

picture
[píktʃər]

v. 마음에 그리다, 상상하다; (그림으로) 그리다, 묘사하다; n. 그림, 사진
If you picture something in your mind, you think of it and have such a clear memory or idea of it that you seem to be able to see it.

strip
[strip]

n. 좁고 긴 땅; 길고 가느다란 조각; v. 벗다, 벗기다, 떼어내다
A strip of land or water is a long narrow area of it.

fist**
[fist]

n. (쥔) 주먹
Your hand is referred to as your fist when you have bent your fingers in towards the palm in order to hit someone, to make an angry gesture, or to hold something.

announce^{까습}
[ənáuns]

vt. 알리다, 공고하다, 전하다
If you announce a piece of news or an intention, especially something that people may not like, you say it loudly and clearly, so that everyone you are with can hear it.

injure*
[índʒər]

vt. 상처를 입히다, 해치다
If you injure a person or animal, you damage some part of their body.

faithful**
[féiθfəl]

a. 충실한, 성실한
Someone who is faithful to a person, organization, idea, or activity remains firm in their belief in them or support for them.

mourn**
[mɔːrn]

v. 슬퍼하다, 한탄하다
If you mourn someone who has died or mourn for them, you are very sad that they have died and show your sorrow in the way that you behave.

carve**
[kɑːrv]

vt. 새기다, 조각하다
If you carve an object, you make it by cutting it out of a substance such as wood or stone.

trunk**
[trʌŋk]

n. 여행 가방; (나무의) 줄기, 몸뚱이
A trunk is a large, strong case or box used for storing things or for taking on a journey.

embroider*
[embrɔ́idər]

v. 수를 놓다, 자수하다, 장식하다
If something such as clothing or cloth is embroidered with a design, the design is stitched into it.

unworn
[ʌnwɔ́ːrn]

a. 한 번도 입지 않은; 닳지 않은, 해어지지 않은
un (반대, 부정의 접두사) + worn (a. 입은)

celebrate**
[séləbrèit]

v. 기념하다, 축하하다
If you celebrate, you do something enjoyable because of a special occasion.

engagement**
[engéidʒmənt]

n. 약혼; 약속, 계약
An engagement is an agreement that two people have made with each other to get married.

soft-spoken
[sɔ́(:)ftspóukən]

a. (말씨가) 부드러운, 상냥한
Someone who is soft-spoken has a quiet, gentle voice.

**look
forward to**

phrasal v. …을 기대하다, 고대하다
If you say that someone is looking forward to something useful or positive, you mean they expect it to happen.

marriage*
[mǽridʒ]

n. 결혼, 혼인
A marriage is the relationship between a husband and wife.

fiancé
[fiːɑːnséi]

n. 약혼자 (남자)
A woman's fiancé is the man to whom she is engaged to be married.

a great deal

idiom 다량, 상당량, 많이
A great deal of something is a large number or amount or extent it.

tease**
[tiːz]

v. 놀리다, 골리다, 괴롭히다; n. 골리기, 놀림
To tease someone means to laugh at them or make jokes about them in order to embarrass, annoy, or upset them.

tickle*
[tíkəl]

vt. 간지럼을 태우다, 간질이다; n. 간지럼
When you tickle someone, you move your fingers lightly over a sensitive part of their body, often in order to make them laugh.

prank*
[præŋk]

n. 농담, 희롱, (짓궂은) 장난
A prank is a childish trick.

nonsense**
[nɑ́nsens]

a. 어리석은, 무의미한; n. 바보 같은 짓; 허튼소리
If you say that something spoken or written is nonsense, you mean that you consider it to be untrue or silly.

shriek**
[ʃriːk]

v. 새된 소리를 지르다, 비명을 지르다; n. 비명
When someone shrieks, they make a short, very loud cry.

linger**
[líŋgər]

vi. 오래 머무르다, 떠나지 못하다
If you linger somewhere, you stay there for a longer time than is necessary, for example because you are enjoying yourself.

defeat*
[difít]

vt. 좌절시키다; 쳐부수다, 패배시키다; n. 패배
If a task or a problem defeats you, it is so difficult that you cannot do it or solve it.

recite**
[risáit]

vt. 읊다, 암송하다; 낭독[낭송]하다
If you recite something such as a list, you say it aloud.

thumb**
[θʌm]

n. 엄지손가락; v. (책을) 엄지손가락으로 넘기다
Your thumb is the short thick part on the side of your hand next to your four fingers.

3.
Where Is Mrs. Hirsch?

1. What was the previous winter like in Copenhagen?

    (A) It was mild and people used wood to heat their homes.
    (B) It was very cold but people had enough fuel for their homes.
    (C) There was no fuel for homes and the nights were very cold.
    (D) The nights were cold but the people could use electricity in their
    houses at night.

2. Why was Annemarie sure that the sign on the Hirsch's store
    was German?

    (A) She learned German in school and could read the sign.
    (B) She saw two German soldiers put the sign on the door.
    (C) She saw a swastika on the sign.
    (D) She didn't know what language the writing was.

3. Annemarie was frightened about Peter being at her
    apartment at night because _____.

    (A) she hadn't seen Peter in a long time
    (B) Copenhagen had a curfew at night
    (C) Peter reminded her of Lise
    (D) Peter scared Annemarie with stories about the war

4. According to Peter, why had he NOT visited Annemarie's family in a long time?

   (A) His work takes him too many different places.

   (B) He was arrested by German soldiers.

   (C) He went on a vacation to the seaside.

   (D) He was busy working at an office in Copenhagen.

5. The Hirsch's store was closed because _____.

   (A) they broke the law so their store was closed down

   (B) they went to the seaside for a family vacation

   (C) they were Jewish and the Germans decided to close down stores run by Jewish people

   (D) they were not making enough money to keep the store open

6. Annemarie thought that the Danish people needed to

   _____.

   (A) obey the German soldiers

   (B) become body guards for the Jewish people in Denmark

   (C) start a war against the Germans

   (D) attack the German soldiers on the streets

7. Annemarie told herself that _____.

   (A) the war would be over soon

   (B) the King of Denmark wouldn't need her help

   (C) she would never be in danger

   (D) ordinary people like her would never be called upon for courage

1분에 몇 단어를 읽는지 리딩 속도를 측정해보세요.

$$\frac{1{,}863 \text{ words}}{\text{reading time ( ) sec}} \times 60 = (\qquad) \text{ WPM}$$

✿ *Build Your Vocabulary*

dawdle
[dɔ́:dl]

v. 꾸물거리다, 빈둥거리다
If you dawdle, you spend more time than is necessary going somewhere.

scamper[*]
[skǽmpər]

vi. 재빨리 달리다, 날쌔게 움직이다
When people or small animals scamper somewhere, they move there quickly with small, light steps.

mitten[*]
[mítn]

n. 벙어리장갑
Mittens are gloves which have one section that covers your thumb and another section that covers your four fingers together.

fuel[**]
[fjú:əl]

n. 연료; v. 연료를 공급하다
Fuel is a substance such as coal, oil, or petrol that is burned to provide heat or power.

chimney[**]
[tʃímni]

n. 굴뚝
A chimney is a pipe through which smoke goes up into the air, usually through the roof of a building.

install[**]
[instɔ́:l]

vt. 설치하다, 장치하다
If you install a piece of equipment, you fit it or put it somewhere so that it is ready to be used.

coal[***]
[koul]

n. 석탄
Coal is a hard black substance that is extracted from the ground and burned as fuel.

ration[*]
[rǽʃən]

vt. 배급을 주다, 제한하다; n. 배급(량)
When something is rationed by a person or government, you are only allowed to have a limited amount of it, usually because there is not enough of it.

frustration[*]
[frʌstréiʃən]

n. 좌절, 실패; 낙담, 좌절감
Frustration is the feeling of being annoyed and impatient because you cannot do or achieve what you want.

dim[복습]
[dim]

a. 어둑한, 흐릿한, 희미한; v. 어둑하게 하다, 흐려지다
Dim light is not bright.

tidy[**]
[táidi]

v. 치우다, 정돈하다; a. 단정한, 말쑥한, 깔끔한
When you tidy a place such as a room or cupboard, you make it neat by putting things in their proper places.

snuggle^{복습}
[snʌ́gəl]

v. 바싹 파고들다, 달라붙다, 끌어안다
If you snuggle somewhere, you settle yourself into a warm, comfortable position, especially by moving closer to another person.

**crib*
[krib]

n. 유아용 침대; 여물통
A crib is a bed for a small baby.

hesitate^{복습}
[hézətèit]

v. 주저하다, 머뭇거리다, 망설이다
If you hesitate, you do not speak or act for a short time, usually because you are uncertain, embarrassed, or worried about what you are going to say or do.

glance^{복습}
[glæns]

v. 흘긋 보다, 잠깐 보다; n. 흘긋 봄
If you glance at something or someone, you look at them very quickly and then look away again immediately.

wet the bed

idiom (잠자리에) 오줌을 싸다
If people, especially children, wet their beds, they urinate in their beds usually during sleeping, because they cannot stop themselves.

haughty*
[hɔ́ːti]

a. 오만한, 거만한 (haughtily ad. 오만하게)
You use haughty to describe someone's behavior or appearance when you disapprove of the fact that they seem to be very proud and to think that they are better than other people.

doorway^{복습}
[dɔ́ːrwèi]

n. 문간, 현관, 출입구
A doorway is a space in a wall where a door opens and closes.

kneel*
[niːl]

vi. (knelt-knelt) 무릎 꿇다
When you kneel, you bend your legs so that your knees are touching the ground.

cheek^{복습}
[tʃiːk]

n. 뺨, 볼
Your cheeks are the sides of your face below your eyes.

thread^{복습}
[θred]

n. 실, 바느질 실; vt. 실을 꿰다
A thread is a long very thin piece of a material such as cotton, nylon, or silk, especially one that is used in sewing.

padlock
[pǽdlàk]

n. 맹꽁이자물쇠; vt. 맹꽁이자물쇠를 채우다
A padlock is a lock which is used for fastening two things together.

giggle*
[gígəl]

v. 낄낄 웃다; n. 낄낄 웃음
If someone giggles, they laugh in a childlike way, because they are amused, nervous, or embarrassed.

make a face^{복습}

idiom 얼굴을 찌푸리다, 침울한 표정을 짓다
If you make a face, you twist your face to indicate a certain mental or emotional state.

stoop*
[stuːp]

v. 웅크리다, 상체를 굽히다, 구부리다 (stooped a. 구부정한)
If you stoop, you bend your body forwards and downwards.

unruly
[ʌnrúːli]

a. (머리털 등이) 흐트러지기 쉬운, 다루기 힘든, 제멋대로 구는
Unruly hair is difficult to keep tidy.

squint*
[skwint]

v. 곁눈질을 하다, 실눈으로 보다; a. 사시의; 곁눈질하는
If you squint at something, you look at it with your eyes partly closed.

wrinkle**
[ríŋkəl]

v. 주름이 지게 하다, 구겨지다; n. 주름, 잔주름
When you wrinkle your nose or forehead, or when it wrinkles, you tighten the muscles in your face so that the skin folds.

nudge
[nʌdʒ]

vt. (물건을) 조금씩[슬쩍] 움직이다; (주의를 끌기 위해 팔꿈치로) 슬쩍 찌르다
If you nudge someone or something into a place or position, you gently push them there.

rubber**
[rʌ́bər]

n. 고무; a. 고무의
Rubber is a strong, waterproof, elastic substance made from the juice of a tropical tree or produced chemically.

creak*
[kri:k]

v. 삐걱삐걱 소리를 내며 움직이(게 하)다; n. 삐걱거리는 소리
If something creaks, it makes a short, high-pitched sound when it moves.

clatter**
[klǽtər]

v. 달가닥달가닥 울리다, 달그락거리며 가다; n. 달가닥하는 소리
If you say that people or things clatter somewhere, you mean that they move there noisily.

seashore**
[síːʃɔ̀ːr]

n. 해변, 해안; a. 해안[해변]의
The seashore is the part of a coast where the land slopes down into the sea.

sarcastic**
[saːrkǽstik]

a. 빈정대는, 비꼬는, 풍자적인 (sarcastically ad. 빈정대며, 비꼬아서)
Someone who is sarcastic says or does the opposite of what they really mean in order to mock or insult someone.

dumb**
[dʌm]

a. (구어) 멍청한, 우둔한; 벙어리의, 말을 하지 않는
If you call a person dumb, you mean that they are stupid or foolish.

reassure복습
[rìːəʃúər]

vt. 안심시키다
If you reassure someone, you say or do things to make them stop worrying about something.

distract*
[distrǽkt]

vt. (마음·주의를) 흐트러뜨리다, 딴 데로 돌리다
(distracted a. (주의가) 빗나간, 마음이 산란한)
If something distracts you or your attention from something, it takes your attention away from it.

peel**
[piːl]

v. 껍질을 벗기다, 벗겨지다
When you peel fruit or vegetables, you remove their skins.

puzzle**
[pʌ́zl]

v. 어리둥절하게 만들다, 곤혹스럽게 하다, 난처하게 하다
(puzzled a. 당혹스러운, 어리둥절한)
If something puzzles you, you do not understand it and feel confused.

grunt*
[grʌnt]

vi. (사람이) 툴툴거리다; (돼지가) 꿀꿀거리다; n. 꿀꿀[툴툴]거리는 소리
If you grunt, you make a low sound, especially because you are annoyed or not interested in something.

frighten ^{복습}
[fráitn]

v. 놀라게 하다, 섬뜩하게 하다; 기겁하다 (frightening a. 무서운)
If something or someone frightens you, they cause you to suddenly feel afraid, anxious, or nervous.

curfew
[kə́:rfju:]

n. 통행금지령, 통금시간
A curfew is a law stating that people must stay inside their houses after a particular time at night, for example during a war.

put one's finger on

idiom ···을 확실히[분명히] 지적하다
If you put your finger on something, for example a reason or problem, you see and identify exactly what it is.

treat ***
[tri:t]

n. 만족[즐거움]을 주는 것, 맛있는 간식; 대접, 환대; vt. 다루다, 대우하다
If you say, for example, that something looks or works a treat, you mean that it looks very good or works very well.

bare ***
[bɛər]

a. 벌거벗은, 있는 그대로의; 텅 빈 (barefoot a. 맨발의)
If a part of your body is bare, it is not covered by any clothing.

grin **
[grin]

v. (이를 드러내고) 싱긋 웃다, 활짝 웃다; n. 싱긋 웃음
When you grin, you smile broadly.

ruffle *
[rʌ́fəl]

v. 구기다, 헝클다; (마음을) 흐트러뜨리다
If you ruffle someone's hair, you move your hand backwards and forwards through it as a way of showing your affection towards them.

footrace
[futreis]

n. 도보(徒步) 경주, 뜀박질 경주
foot (n. 발) + race (n. 경주)

seashell
[sí:ʃèl]

n. 조개껍질
Seashells are the empty shells of small sea creatures.

ridge **
[ridʒ]

v. (표면을) 이랑처럼 만들다; n. 산등성이, 산마루 (ridged a. 이랑 모양이 된)
A ridged surface has raised lines on it.

pearly
[pə́:rli]

a. 진주의, 진주 같은, 진주색의
Something that is pearly is pale and shines softly, like a pearl.

practical ***
[prǽktikəl]

a. 실용적인; 실제의, 실제적인
Practical ideas and methods are likely to be effective or successful in a real situation.

sip ^{복습}
[sip]

n. 한 모금; v. 찔끔찔끔 마시다
A sip is a small amount of drink that you take into your mouth.

issue ***
[íʃu:]

v. 내다, 발하다, 발행하다; n. 발행; 논쟁점
If you issue a statement or a warning, you make it known formally or publicly.

torment **
[tɔ́:rment]

vt. 괴롭히다, 고문하다; n. 고통, 고뇌
If something torments you, it causes you extreme mental suffering.

dope *
[doup]

n. (구어) 멍청이; (속어) 마약
If someone calls a person a dope, they think that the person is stupid.

drawn***
[drɔ:n]

a. 찡그린, 일그러진; DRAW(v. 그리다; 빼다, 당기다)의 과거분사
If someone or their face looks drawn, their face is thin and they look very tired, ill, worried, or unhappy.

keep an eye on

idiom …을 감시하다, 주목하다
If you keep an eye on someone or something, you watch them or it carefully.

shrug*
[ʃrʌg]

v. (양 손바닥을 내보이면서 어깨를) 으쓱하다; n. 으쓱하기
If you shrug, you raise your shoulders to show that you are not interested in something or that you do not know or care about something.

incident***
[ínsədənt]

n. 일어난 일, 작은 사건
An incident is something that happens, often something that is unpleasant.

cocoon
[kəkú:n]

n. 안식처, 보호막; 누에고치
If you are in a cocoon of something, you are wrapped up in it or surrounded by it.

Dane***
[dein]

n. 덴마크 사람
A Dane is a person who comes from Denmark.

fairy tale***
[fɛ́əritèil]

n. 동화, 옛날이야기
A fairy tale is a story for children involving magical events and imaginary creatures.

call upon

phrasal v. …에게 (…을) 청하다, 요구하다
If you call on someone to do something or call upon them to do it, you say publicly that you want them to do it.

courageous**
[kəréidʒəs]

a. 용기 있는, 용감한, 담력이 있는
Someone who is courageous shows courage.

ordinary***
[ɔ́:rdənèri]

a. 보통의, 평범한
Ordinary people or things are normal and not special or different in any way.

4.
It Will Be a Long Night

1. Why did Kirsti get fish shoes?

   (A) Her mother could not afford leather shoes.

   (B) Kirsti wanted fish shoes because they were green.

   (C) There was no leather available in Copenhagen.

   (D) Kirsti liked shiny black shoes.

2. Why did Annemarie and Ellen play with Kirsti in the apartment?

   (A) Annemarie and Ellen always enjoyed playing with Kirsti.

   (B) Annemarie and Ellen needed another character to play *Gone With the Wind*.

   (C) Annemarie would be scolded if she did not let Kirsti to play with her.

   (D) Ellen wanted Kirsti to be her daughter when playing *Gone With the Wind*.

3. Why was Tivoli Gardens closed?

   (A) No Danish people could afford to visit the gardens during the war.

   (B) The German soldiers used the gardens as a military base.

   (C) The Danish people closed the gardens so German soldiers could not visit the gardens.

   (D) The German soldiers burned down part of the garden.

4. Why was the Danish naval fleet destroyed?

   (A) The German soldiers destroyed the Danish naval fleet.

   (B) The Danish naval fleet was destroyed by Swedish people.

   (C) The Danish naval fleet was destroyed in a fight against the
   Germans.

   (D) The Danish people destroyed their own naval fleet
   so that the Germans could not use the ships.

5. How did the Germans get information about the Jewish
   people in Copenhagen?

   (A) The Germans took the list of names from the synagogue.

   (B) The Jewish people in Copenhagen told the Germans they were
   Jewish.

   (C) The German soldiers searched every apartment in Copenhagen
   looking for Jewish people.

   (D) The Danish government told the German soldiers where Jewish
   people lived.

6. Annemarie's father promised Ellen _____.

   (A) she would be safe

   (B) her parents were safe

   (C) he would trick the German soldiers

   (D) the war would end soon

7. What would the Johansen family do if the Germans came
   to their apartment?

   (A) They would secretly leave their apartment in the night.

   (B) They would hide Ellen in their apartment.

   (C) They would pretend that Annemarie and Ellen were sisters.

   (D) They would give Ellen to the German soldiers.

1분에 몇 단어를 읽는지 리딩 속도를 측정해보세요.

$$\frac{2{,}375 \text{ words}}{\text{reading time (} \qquad \text{) sec}} \times 60 = (\qquad) \text{ WPM}$$

✿ *Build Your Vocabulary*

sprawl*
[sprɔːl]

v. (팔다리 등을) 쭉 펴다, 큰 대자로 눕다; 퍼져 나가다, 넓은 지역에 걸치다
If you sprawl somewhere, you sit or lie down with your legs and arms spread out in a careless way.

old-fashioned**
[óuldfǽʃənd]

a. 구식의, 유행에 뒤떨어진
Old-fashioned ideas, customs, or values are the ideas, customs, and values of the past.

rug**
[rʌg]

n. (방바닥 · 마루에 까는) 깔개, 융단
A rug is a piece of thick material that you put on a floor.

ball별도
[bɔːl]

① n. 무도회, 댄스파티 ② n. 공, 공 모양의 것
A ball is a large formal social event at which people dance.

sophisticated*
[səfístəkèitid]

a. 세련된, 교양 있는; 세상에 밝은, 박식한
Someone who is sophisticated is comfortable in social situations and knows about culture, fashion, and other matters that are considered socially important.

performer*
[pərfɔ́ːrmər]

n. 연기자, 연주자; 실행하는 사람
A performer is a person who acts, sings, or does other entertainment in front of audiences.

dramatics
[drəmǽtiks]

n. 아마추어 연극; 연출법, 연기술
You use dramatics to refer to activities connected with the theater and drama, such as acting in plays or producing them.

stomp
[stamp]

v. 쿵쿵거리며 걷다, 발을 구르다
If you stomp somewhere, you walk there with very heavy steps, often because you are angry.

tear-stained
[tíərstèind]

a. 눈물에 젖은, 눈물 어린
tear (n. 눈물) + stained (a. 얼룩진)

glower
[gláuər]

vi. 노려보다, 쏘아보다, 불쾌한 얼굴을 하다
If you glower at someone or something, you look at them angrily.

exasperate*
[igzǽspərèit]

vt. 성나게 하다, 격분시키다 (exasperated a. 화가 치민)
If something exasperates you, they annoy you and make you feel frustrated or upset.

sputter*
[spʌ́tər]

v. 흥분하여 말하다, 식식거리며 말하다; 푸푸[지글지글, 탁탁] 소리를 내다
If you sputter, you speak with difficulty and make short sounds, especially because you are angry, shocked, or excited.

chain***
[tʃein]
v. 사슬로 매다; n. 쇠사슬; 연쇄, 일련
If a person or thing is chained to something, they are fastened to it with a chain.

beat^{복습}
[bi:t]
v. 치다, 두드리다; 패배시키다, 이기다; (심장, 맥박 등이) 뛰다; n. [음악] 박자, 고동
If you beat someone or something, you hit them very hard.

giggle^{복습}
[gígəl]
v. 낄낄 웃다; n. 낄낄 웃음
If someone giggles, they laugh in a childlike way, because they are amused, nervous, or embarrassed.

questioning
[kwéstʃəniŋ]
a. 따지는, 캐묻는; n. 의문, 질문 (questioningly ad. 질문조로, 미심쩍게)
If someone has a questioning expression on their face, they look as if they want to know the answer to a question.

outgrow
[áutgróu]
v. (outgrew-outgrown) …보다 더 커지다, 너무 커져 맞지 않게 되다
If a child outgrows a piece of clothing, they grow bigger, so that it no longer fits them.

bellow*
[bélou]
v. 고함지르다, 우렁찬 소리를 내다; n. 울부짖는 소리, 고함소리
If someone bellows, they shout angrily in a loud, deep voice.

soothing
[sú:ðiŋ]
a. 달래는, 위로하는, 진정시키는 (soothingly ad. 달래며, 위로하며)
Something that is soothing has a calming, assuaging, or relieving effect.

sniff**
[snif]
v. 콧방귀를 뀌다; 코를 킁킁거리다, 냄새를 맡다; n. 냄새 맡음; 콧방귀
When you sniff, you breathe in air through your nose hard enough to make a sound, for example when you are trying not to cry, or in order to show disapproval.

disgust**
[disgΛst]
n. 싫음, 혐오감; vt. 역겹게 하다, 넌더리나게 하다
Disgust is a feeling of very strong dislike or disapproval.

leather^{복습}
[léðər]
n. 가죽
Leather is treated animal skin which is used for making shoes, clothes, bags, and furniture.

odd-looking
[ádlùkiŋ]
a. 괴상하게 보이는
If you describe someone or something as odd-looking, you think that they look strange or unusual.

scale**
[skeil]
① n. 비늘 ② n. 규모; 비례, 비율; v. 기어오르다 ③ n. 저울 접시, 저울
The scales of a fish or reptile are the small, flat pieces of hard skin that cover its body.

wail^{복습}
[weil]
v. (큰소리로) 투덜거리다; 울부짖다, 통곡하다; n. 울부짖음, 비탄, 한탄
If you wail something, you say it in a loud, high-pitched voice that shows that you are unhappy or in pain.

frown**
[fraun]
vi. 얼굴을 찡그리다, 눈살을 찌푸리다; n. 찌푸린 얼굴
When someone frowns, their eyebrows become drawn together, because they are annoyed or puzzled.

improve***
[imprú:v]
v. 개선하다, 진보하다, 나아지다 (improvement n. 개선, 향상)
If something improves or if you improve it, it gets better.

ponder*
[pándər]

v. 숙고하다, 깊이 생각하다
If you ponder something, you think about it carefully.

disdainful
[disdéinfəl]

a. 업신여기는, 무시하는, 거드름 부리는 (disdainfully ad. 거드름 부리며)
To be disdainful means to dislike something or someone because you think they are unimportant or not worth your attention.

squat*
[skwɑt]

v. 웅크리다, 쪼그리고 앉다; a. 땅딸막한, 쪼그리고 앉은
If you squat, you lower yourself towards the ground, balancing on your feet with your legs bent.

pest*
[pest]

n. 골칫거리, 성가신 것; 해충; 페스트(병)
You can describe someone, especially a child, as a pest if they keep bothering you.

butt*
[bʌt]

v. (머리로) 들이받다, 부딪히다; n. 뭉툭한 끝 부분; (구어) 엉덩이
(butt in phrasal v. …에 참견하다, 주제넘게 나서다)
If you say that someone is butting in, you are criticizing the fact that they are joining in a conversation or activity without being asked to.

scold牧會
[skould]

v. 꾸짖다, 잔소리하다
If you scold someone, you speak angrily to them because they have done something wrong.

twirl*
[twəːrl]

v. 빠르게 돌다, 빙빙 돌리다; n. 회전, 비틀어 돌림
If you twirl something or if it twirls, it turns around and around with a smooth, fairly fast movement.

firework*
[fáiərwə̀ːrk]

n. 불꽃, 불꽃놀이
Fireworks are small objects that are lit to entertain people on special occasions.

carousel
[kèrusél]

n. 회전목마
A carousel is a large circular machine with seats, often in the shape of animals or cars. People can sit on it and go round and round for fun.

designate**
[dézignèit]

vt. 지명하다, 지정하다, 선정하다, 명시하다
When you designate someone or something as a particular thing, you formally give them that description or name.

magnificent**
[mægnífəsənt]

a. 웅장한, 장엄한, 훌륭한
If you say that something or someone is magnificent, you mean that you think they are extremely good, beautiful, or impressive.

splash**
[splæʃ]

n. (잉크 등의) 튄 물, 방울, 얼룩; v. (물·흙탕 등) 튀(기)다, 첨벙거리다
A splash of color is an area of a bright color which contrasts strongly with the colors around it.

burst***
[bəːrst]

n. 폭발, 파열; 돌발; v. 갑자기 …하다; 파열하다, 터지다
A burst of something is a sudden short period of it.

best of all

idiom 무엇보다도 가장 좋은
You use best of all to indicate that what you are about to mention is the thing that you prefer or that has most advantages out of all the things you have mentioned.

scoff*
[skɔːf]

v. 비웃다, 조소하다, 조롱하다; n. 비웃음, 조롱
If you scoff at something, you speak about it in a way that shows you think it is ridiculous or inadequate.

occupationᴴᴸ
[àkjəpéiʃən]

n. 점령, 점거; 직업, 업무
The occupation of a country happens when it is entered and controlled by a foreign army.

force***
[fɔːrs]

n. 힘, 폭력, 군사력; vt. 억지로 …시키다, 강요하다
The force of something is the powerful effect or quality that it has.

punish**
[pʌ́niʃ]

v. 벌하다, 응징하다, 처벌하다
To punish someone means to make them suffer in some way because they have done something wrong.

lighthearted
[láithɑ́ːrtid]

a. 근심 걱정 없는, 마음 편한; 쾌활한, 명랑한
Someone who is lighthearted is cheerful and happy.

stiffᴴᴸ
[stif]

a. 굳은, 뻣뻣한; 완강한, 완고한
Something that is stiff is firm or does not bend easily.

belligerent*
[bəlídʒərənt]

a. 적대적인, 공격적인 (belligerently ad. 적대적으로, 호전적으로)
A belligerent person is hostile and aggressive.

boom**
[buːm]

n. 쿵 하는 소리; 대유행, 붐; v. 쿵 하고 울리다; 번창하다
When something such as someone's voice, a cannon, or a big drum booms, it makes a loud, deep sound that lasts for several seconds.

explosion**
[iksplóuʒən]

n. 폭발, 파열
An explosion is a sudden, violent burst of energy, for example one caused by a bomb.

ablaze
[əbléiz]

a. 불길에 휩싸인
Something that is ablaze is burning very fiercely.

celebration**
[sèləbréiʃən]

n. 축하, 축전, 기념행사
A celebration is a special enjoyable event that people organize because something pleasant has happened.

naval **
[néivəl]

a. 해군의, 해군에 의한
Naval means belonging to, relating to, or involving a country's navy.

fleet*
[fliːt]

n. 함대, 선단
A fleet is a group of ships organized to do something together, for example to fight battles or to catch fish.

blow***
[blou]

v. 폭파하다; 불다, 바람에 날리다; n. 불기, 강풍
To blow something out, off, or away means to remove or destroy it violently with an explosion.

vessel***
[vésəl]

n. (큰) 배, 선박; 용기, 그릇
A vessel is a ship or large boat.

navy**
[néivi]

n. 해군; 짙은 남색
A country's navy consists of the people it employs to fight at sea, and the ships they use.

submerge*
[səbmə́:rdʒ]

v. 물속에 잠기다, 침몰하다
If something submerges or if you submerge it, it goes below the surface of some water or another liquid.

harbor***
[háːrbər]

n. 항구, 항만
A harbor is an area of the sea at the coast which is partly enclosed by land or strong walls, so that boats can be left there safely.

awe**
[ɔː]

vt. 경외심을 갖게 하다; n. 경외, 외경심 (awed a. 외경심에 휩싸인)
If you are awed by someone or something, they make you feel respectful and amazed, though often rather frightened.

chatterbox
[tʃǽtərbɑ̀ks]

n. 수다쟁이
A chatterbox is someone who talks a lot.

tense*
[tens]

a. 긴장한; 긴박한; 팽팽한; v. 긴장시키다[하다], 팽팽하게 하다
A tense situation or period of time is one that makes people anxious, because they do not know what is going to happen next.

clap**
[klæp]

v. 박수를 치다; 가볍게 치다[두드리다]
When you clap, you hit your hands together to show appreciation or attract attention.

dismay*
[disméi]

n. 낙담, 실망, 경악; vt. 낙담[실망하게 하다
Dismay is a strong feeling of fear, worry, or sadness that is caused by something unpleasant and unexpected.

roast**
[roust]

v. 굽다, 그을리다, 뜨겁게 하다
When you roast meat or other food, you cook it by dry heat in an oven or over a fire.

brisk**
[brisk]

a. 활발한, 활기찬, 기운찬; v. 활기를 띠(게 하)다 (briskly ad. 활발하게)
A brisk activity or action is done quickly and in an energetic way.

relative**
[rélətiv]

n. 친척; a. 상대적인, 관계가 있는
Your relatives are the members of your family.

pout***
[paut]

v. 입을 삐죽거리다, 토라지다; n. 입을 삐죽거림, 뿌루퉁한 얼굴
If someone pouts, they stick out their lips, in order to show that they are annoyed.

argue**
[áːrgjuː]

v. 논쟁하다, 주장하다
If one person argues with another, they speak angrily to each other about something that they disagree about.

dubious*
[djúːbiəs]

a. 수상쩍은, 의심스러운; 모호한, 애매한 (dubiously ad. 의심스러워하며)
If you are dubious about something, you are not completely sure about it and have not yet made up your mind about it.

helping
[hélpiŋ]

n. (음식의) 한 그릇; 조력, 원조 (second helping n. 두 그릇째)
A helping of food is the amount of it that you get in a single serving.

tension[*]
[ténʃən]

n. 긴장, 불안
Tension is a feeling of worry and anxiety which makes it difficult for you to relax.

chatter[*]
[tʃǽtər]

v. 수다를 떨다, 재잘거리다; 지저귀다
If you chatter, you talk quickly and continuously, usually about things which are not important.

stroke[*]
[strouk]

① vt. 쓰다듬다, 어루만지다; n. 쓰다듬기, 달램 ② n. 타격, 일격, 치기
If you stroke someone or something, you move your hand slowly and gently over them.

congregation[*]
[kàŋgrigéiʃən]

n. (교회의) 신자[신도]들; (종교적인) 집회, 모임, 회합
The people who are attending a church service or who regularly attend a church service are referred to as the congregation.

arrest[***]
[ərést]

vt. 체포하다, 저지하다; n. 체포, 검거, 구속
If the police arrest you, they take charge of you and take you to a police station, because they believe you may have committed a crime.

relocation
[rìːloukéiʃən]

n. 재배치, 배치 전환
Relocation is the transportation of people to a new settlement.

stun[*]
[stʌn]

vt. 어리벙벙하게 하다; 기절시키다; n. 놀라게 함
If you are stunned by something, you are extremely shocked or surprised by it and are therefore unable to speak or do anything.

sob[**]
[sɑb]

v. 흐느껴 울다; n. 흐느낌, 오열
When someone sobs, they cry in a noisy way, breathing in short breaths.

hesitate[*]
[hézətèit]

v. 주저하다, 머뭇거리다, 망설이다
If you hesitate, you do not speak or act for a short time, usually because you are uncertain, embarrassed, or worried about what you are going to say or do.

stuff[***]
[stʌf]

vt. 채워 넣다, 속을 채우다; n. 물건, 물질 (stuffed a. 속을 채운)
If you stuff a container or space with something, you fill it with something or with a quantity of things until it is full.

interrupt[*]
[ìntərʌ́pt]

v. 방해하다, 가로막다, 저지하다
If you interrupt someone who is speaking, you say or do something that causes them to stop.

terrify[**]
[térəfài]

vt. 무섭게[겁나게] 하다, 놀래다 (terrified a. 무서워하는, 겁에 질린)
If something terrifies you, it makes you feel extremely frightened.

braid[*]
[breid]

vt. (머리·끈 등을) 땋다; n. 땋은 끈, 땋은 머리
If you braid hair or a group of threads, you twist three or more lengths of the hair or threads over and under each other to make one thick length.

pigtail[*]
[pígtèil]

n. 땋아 늘인 머리 (돼지 꼬리와 비슷한 모양에서 유래)
If someone has a pigtail or pigtails, their hair is plaited or braided into one or two lengths.

5.
Who Is the Dark-Haired One?

1. The Johansens kept Lise's things _____.

   (A) under Annemarie's bed

   (B) in a blue trunk in Annemarie's room

   (C) in a box in Kirsti's bedroom

   (D) in a suitcase in the living room

2. Why did the German soldiers come to the Johansen's apartment at night?

   (A) They thought that the Johansens were hiding the Rosens.

   (B) They thought that the Johansens were helping the Resistance fighters.

   (C) They wanted to ask Mr. Johansen about his business.

   (D) They saw the Johansens lights on after curfew.

3. Why did Annemarie pull the gold necklace off of Ellen's neck before the German soldiers saw her?

   (A) The German soldiers would steal her necklace if they saw it.

   (B) The necklace had the Star of David on it and the soldiers would know that Ellen was Jewish.

   (C) No women or children were allowed to wear jewelry during the war.

   (D) The necklace was caught in Ellen's hair and it wouldn't come loose.

4. The German soldiers who came to Annemarie's apartment were _____ than the soldiers on the streets.

   (A) younger and angrier
   (B) friendlier and older
   (C) wearing different uniforms
   (D) older and angrier

5. Why didn't the soldiers believe that Ellen was Annemarie's sister?

   (A) Ellen's eyes were not the same color as Annemarie's eyes.
   (B) Ellen had dark hair.
   (C) Ellen did not look like the Johansens.
   (D) Ellen and Annemarie looked the same age.

6. What did Papa show the soldiers to convince them that Ellen was his child?

   (A) All of the pictures from the family photo album.
   (B) Lise's birth certificate.
   (C) A baby photo of Lise.
   (D) Ellen's baby picture.

7. What did the German soldier do with photo of Lise?

   (A) He dropped it on a hot stove.
   (B) He put it in his coat pocket.
   (C) He tore it in half.
   (D) He burned it with a match.

1분에 몇 단어를 읽는지 리딩 속도를 측정해보세요.

$$\frac{2{,}181 \text{ words}}{\text{reading time (\quad) sec}} \times 60 = (\qquad) \text{ WPM}$$

✿ *Build Your Vocabulary*

hook**
[huk]

n. 갈고리, 훅, 걸쇠; v. 갈고리로 걸다
A hook is a bent piece of metal or plastic that is used for catching or holding things, or for hanging things up.

pretend^{복습}
[priténd]

v. ···인 체하다, 가장하다; a. 가짜의, 꾸민
If you pretend that something is the case, you act in a way that is intended to make people believe that it is the case, although in fact it is not.

tiptoe**
[típtòu]

n. 발끝; vi. 발끝으로 걷다, 발돋움하다
If you do something on tiptoe or on tiptoes, you do it standing or walking on the front part of your foot, without putting your heels on the ground.

convince**
[kənvíns]

vt. 설득하다, 확신시키다, 납득시키다
If someone or something convinces you of something, they make you believe that it is true or that it exists.

imperious*
[impíəriəs]

a. 오만한, 거만한, 건방진, 절박한, 긴급한
If you describe someone as imperious, you mean that they have a proud manner and expect to be obeyed.

intone
[intóun]

v. (기도문 등을) 읊조리다
If you intone something, you say it in a slow and serious way, with most of the words at one pitch.

haul**
somebody off
[hɔ:l]

phrasal v. ···를 (강제로) 데려가다, 연행하다, 소환하다
To haul somebody means to force them to go somewhere that they do not want to go, especially to prision.

mental**
[méntl]

a. 정신의, 마음의; 정신병의
Mental means relating to the state or the health of a person's mind.

institution**
[ìnstətjú:ʃən]

n. 시설, 기관, 협회; 제도, 관례
An institution is a building where certain people are looked after, for example people who are mentally ill or children who have no parents.

funeral**
[fjú:nərəl]

n. 장례식
A funeral is the ceremony that is held when the body of someone who has died is buried or cremated.

exact[**] [igzǽkt]

a. 정확한, 정밀한 (exactly ad. 정확하게, 꼭)
Exact means correct in every detail.

confess[**] [kənfés]

v. 자백하다, 고백하다, 인정하다
If someone confesses to doing something wrong, they admit that they did it.

rush[***] [rʌʃ]

v. 급히 움직이다, 서두르다, 돌진하다
If you rush somewhere, you go there quickly.

stay up

phrasal v. 자지 않고 일어나 있다; 그대로 있다
If you stay up, you remain out of bed at a time when most people have gone to bed or at a time when you are normally in bed yourself.

undo[*] [ʌndúː]

v. (undid-undone) 원상태로 돌리다, (묶인 것을) 풀다
To undo something that has been done means to reverse its effect.

braid[복습] [breid]

n. 땋은 끈, 땋은 머리; vt. (머리·끈 등을) 땋다
A braid is a length of hair which has been divided into three or more lengths and then woven together.

slippery[*] [slípəri]

a. 미끄러운, 미끈거리는
Something that is slippery is smooth, wet, or oily and is therefore difficult to walk on or to hold.

fist[복습] [fist]

n. (쥔) 주먹
Your hand is referred to as your fist when you have bent your fingers in towards the palm in order to hit someone, to make an angry gesture, or to hold something.

pound[*] [paund]

① v. 쿵쿵 울리다, 마구 치다, 세게 두드리다; n. 타격 ② n. 파운드(무게의 단위) ③ n. 울타리, 우리
If you pound something or pound on it, you hit it with great force, usually loudly and repeatedly.

slam[*] [slæm]

n. 쾅 (하는 소리); v. (문 따위를) 탕 닫다, 세게 치다; 털썩 내려놓다
A slam is noise made by the forceful impact of two objects.

blow[복습] [blou]

v. (blew-blown) 불다, 바람에 날리다; 폭파하다; n. 불기, 강풍
If you blow, you send out a stream of air from your mouth.

trunk[복습] [trʌŋk]

n. 여행 가방; (나무의) 줄기, 몸통이
A trunk is a large, strong case or box used for storing things or for taking on a journey.

murmur[복습] [mə́ːrmər]

v. 중얼거리다; 투덜거리다; n. 중얼거림
If you murmur something, you say it very quietly, so that not many people can hear what you are saying.

yawn[**] [jɔːn]

n. 하품; vi. 하품하다
Yawn is an act of opening mouth very wide and breathe in more air than usual, often when you are tired or when you are not interested in something.

breeze[**] [briːz]

n. 산들바람, 미풍; vi. 산들산들 불다
A breeze is a gentle wind.

imaginings
[imǽdʒiniŋz]

n. 상상의 산물, 공상, 환상
Imaginings are things that you think you have seen or heard, although actually you have not.

contented*
[kənténtid]

a. 만족한 (contentedly ad. 만족해서, 느긋하게)
If you are contented, you are satisfied with your life or the situation you are in.

abrupt*
[əbrʌ́pt]

a. 갑작스러운, 뜻밖의; 퉁명스러운 (abruptly ad. 갑자기)
An abrupt change or action is very sudden, often in a way which is unpleasant.

ease***
[iːz]

v. 천천히 움직이다; (통증 등이) 가벼워지다, 편해지다; n. 편함, 안정
If you ease your way somewhere or ease somewhere, you move there slowly, carefully, and gently.

crack**
[kræk]

n. 조금, 약간; 갈라진 금; 갑작스런 날카로운 소리; v. 금이 가다, 깨다, 부수다
If you open something such as a door, window, or curtain a crack, you open it only a small amount.

peek
[piːk]

vi. 살짝 들여다보다, 엿보다; n. 엿봄
If you peek at something or someone, you have a quick look at them.

switch**
[switʃ]

v. 스위치를 넣다[돌리다]; n. 스위치
If you switch on an electrical device, a machine or an engine, you start it by pressing a switch or a button.

dare***
[dɛər]

v. 감히 …하다, 무릅쓰다, 도전하다
If you dare to do something, you do something which requires a lot of courage.

strict**
[strikt]

a. 엄격한, 엄한 (strictly ad. 엄격히)
A strict rule or order is very clear and precise or severe and must always be obeyed completely.

ration 복습
[rǽʃən]

vt. 배급을 주다, 제한하다; n. 배급(량)
When something is rationed by a person or government, you are only allowed to have a limited amount of it, usually because there is not enough of it.

startle*
[stáːrtl]

v. 깜짝 놀라게 하다; 움찔하다; n. 깜짝 놀람 (startling a. 깜짝 놀라게 하는)
If something sudden and unexpected startles you, it surprises and frightens you slightly.

make
an effort

idiom 노력하다, 애쓰다
If you make the effort to do something, you do it, even though you need extra energy to do it or you do not really want to.

assume***
[əsjúːm]

vt. 추정하다, 가정하다; (역할 · 임무 등을) 맡다
If you assume that something is true, you imagine that it is true, sometimes wrongly.

stalk*
[stɔːk]

① vi. 활보하다, 으스대며 걷다; 몰래 접근하다 ② n. 줄기, 잎자루
If you stalk somewhere, you walk there in a stiff, proud, or angry way.

sliver
[slívər]

n. 찢어진 조각, 가느다란 조각; vt. 세로로 길게 베다[찢다]
A sliver of something is a small thin piece or amount of it.

holster
[hóulstər]

vt. 권총용 가죽 케이스에 넣다; n. 권총용 가죽 케이스
If you holster something, such as a gun, you put it into a leather case which attaches to a belt, strap, or saddle.

pistol**
[pístl]

n. 권총, 피스톨
A pistol is a small gun which is held in and fired from one hand.

waist**
[weist]

n. 허리
Your waist is the middle part of your body where it narrows slightly above your hips.

peer*
[piər]

vi. 응시하다, 자세히 보다
If you peer at something, you look at it very hard.

blur*
[blə:r]

n. 흐림, 침침함; 더러움, 얼룩; v. (광경·의식·눈 등을) 흐리게 하다
A blur is a shape or area which you cannot see clearly because it has no distinct outline or because it is moving very fast.

object***
[əbdʒékt]

v. 반대하다, 이의를 제기하다; n. [ábdʒikt] 물건, 대상, 목적
If you object to something, you express your dislike or disapproval of it.

harsh^{복습}
[ha:rʃ]

a. (소리 따위가) 귀에 거슬리는; 거친, 가혹한
Harsh voices and sounds are ones that are rough and unpleasant to listen to.

bang**
[bæŋ]

n. 쾅하는 소리; v. 탕 치다, 부딪치다, 쾅 닫(히)다
A bang is a sudden loud noise such as the noise of an explosion.

stumble**
[stʌmbəl]

v. 비틀거리며 걷다, 발부리가 걸리다; n. 비틀거림
If you stumble, you put your foot down awkwardly while you are walking or running and nearly fall over.

urgent**
[ə́:rdʒənt]

a. 다급한, 긴급한, 절박한 (urgently ad. 다급하게)
If something is urgent, it needs to be dealt with as soon as possible.

necklace
[néklis]

n. 목걸이
A necklace is a piece of jewelry such as a chain or a string of beads which someone, usually a woman, wears round their neck.

desperate**
[déspərit]

a. 필사적인; 절망적인, 자포자기의 (desperately a. 필사적으로)
If you are desperate, you are in such a bad situation that you are willing to try anything to change it.

unhook
[ʌnhúk]

v. 갈고리를 벗기다, (의복 등의) 훅을 끄르다
If you unhook something that is held in place by hooks, you open it or remove it by undoing the hooks.

clasp**
[klæsp]

n. 걸쇠, 버클; 악수, 포옹; v. 고정시키다, 죄다; 꼭 쥐다, 악수하다
A clasp is a small device that fastens something.

frantic*
[fræntik]

a. 광란의, 극도로 흥분한 (frantically ad. 미친 듯이)
If you are frantic, you are behaving in a wild and uncontrolled way because you are frightened or worried.

sound asleep

idiom 깊이 잠들어
If someone is sound asleep, they are sleeping very deeply.

yank
[jæŋk]

v. 홱 잡아당기다; n. 홱 잡아당김
If you yank someone or something somewhere, you pull them there suddenly and with a lot of force.

flood*
[flʌd]

v. 범람하다, 넘치다; n. 홍수
If light floods a place or floods into it, it suddenly fills it.

crumple*
[krʌ́mpl]

v. 구기다, 쭈글쭈글하게 하다; 구겨지다; n. 주름
If you crumple something such as paper or cloth, or if it crumples, it is squashed and becomes full of untidy creases and folds.

terrify^{복습}
[térəfài]

vt. 무섭게[겁나게] 하다, 놀래다 (terrified a. 무서워하는, 겁먹은)
If something terrifies you, it makes you feel extremely frightened.

aim*
[əim]

v. 겨냥을 하다, 목표삼다; n. 겨냥, 조준; 목적
If you aim a weapon or object at something or someone, you point it towards them before firing or throwing it.

sweep*
[swi:p]

n. 쓸기, 한 번 휘두름; 청소; v. 휩쓸어 가다, 쓸어내리다
A sweep is a quick smooth movement.

bathrobe
[bǽθroub]

n. 목욕 가운
A bathrobe is a loose piece of clothing made of the same material as towels.

peg*
[peg]

n. 걸이 못, 나무 못, 쐐기
A small stick or hook which sticks out from a surface and from which objects.

chest*
[tʃest]

① n. 상자, 궤 ② n. 가슴; 흉곽
A chest is a large, heavy box used for storing things.

drawer*
[drɔ́:ər]

n. 서랍
A drawer is part of a desk, chest, or other piece of furniture that is shaped like a box and is designed for putting things in.

heap*
[hi:p]

n. 더미, 쌓아올린 것; 덩어리
A heap of things is a pile of them, especially a pile arranged in a rather untidy way.

pile*
[pail]

v. 쌓아 올리다; 쌓이다; n. 쌓아 올린 더미, 다수
If you pile things somewhere, you put them there so that they form a mass of them that is high in the middle and has sloping sides.

rocking chair
[rákiŋtʃèər]

n. 흔들의자
A rocking chair is a chair that is built on two curved pieces of wood so that you can rock yourself backwards and forwards when you are sitting in it.

tremble^{복습}
[trémbəl]

v. 떨다, 떨리다
If you tremble, you shake slightly because you are frightened or cold.

ill at ease

idiom 거북한, 불안한, 불편해 하는
If someone is ill at ease, they are worried and not relaxed.

giraffe수능
[dʒəræf]

n. [동물] 기린
A giraffe is a large African animal with a very long neck, long legs, and dark patches on its body.

bark***
[bɑːrk]

v. 고함치다, 소리 지르며 말하다; 짖다
If you bark at someone, you shout at them aggressively in a loud, rough voice.

glare수능
[glɛər]

v. 노려보다; 번쩍번쩍 빛나다; n. 섬광; 노려봄
If you glare at someone, you look at them with an angry expression on your face.

swallow**
[swɑ́lou]

v. 삼키다, 목구멍으로 넘기다; (초조해서) 마른침을 삼키다
If you swallow, you make a movement in your throat as if you are drinking something, often because you are nervous or frightened.

clear one's throat

idiom (헛)기침하다
If you clear your throat, you cough once in order to make it easier to speak or to attract people's attention.

grim**
[grim]

a. 험상스러운, 무서운; 엄한, 엄격한 (grimly ad. 험악하게)
If a person or their behavior is grim, they are very serious, usually because they are worried about something.

wince*
[wins]

vi. (아픔 · 무서움 때문에) 주춤하다, 움츠리다, 움찔하다
If you wince, you suddenly look as if you are suffering because you feel pain.

scornful*
[skɔ́ːrnfəl]

a. 경멸하는, 조소하는, 업신여기는 (scornfully ad. 깔보며, 경멸적으로)
If you are scornful of someone or something, you show contempt for them.

lock
[lɑk]

① n. 머리채, (머리의) 뭉치 ② n. 자물쇠; v. 자물쇠를 채우다; 고정시키다
A lock of hair is a small bunch of hairs on your head that grow together and curl or curve in the same direction.

treatment**
[tríːtmənt]

n. 취급, 대우, 대접; 치료법, 치료제
Your treatment of someone is the way you behave towards them or deal with them.

sneer수능
[sniər]

n. 비웃음, 냉소; v. 비웃다, 냉소하다
A sneer is a facial expression which shows contempt or scorn.

swift**
[swift]

a. 빠른, 신속한 (swiftly ad. 빨리, 즉시)
A swift event or process happens very quickly or without delay.

tear**
[tɛər]

① v. (tore–torn) 찢다, 찢어지다; n. 찢음 ② n. 눈물
If you tear paper, cloth, or another material, or if it tears, you pull it into two pieces or you pull it so that a hole appears in it.

release**
[rilíːs]

vt. 놓아주다, 해방시키다, 풀어놓다; n. 석방
If you release a device, you move it so that it stops holding something.

contain***
[kəntéin]

vt. 포함하다, 담고 있다; 억누르다, 참다
If writing, speech, or film contains particular information, ideas, or images, it includes them.

portrait**
[pɔ́ːrtrit]

n. 초상, 초상화
A portrait is a painting, drawing, or photograph of a particular person.

infant**
[ínfənt]

n. 유아, 갓난아기; a. 유아(용)의
An infant is a baby or very young child.

delicate**
[délikət]

a. 섬세한, 고운; 예민한, 민감한
Something that is delicate has a color, taste, or smell which is pleasant and not strong or intense.

unwavering
[ʌnwéivəriŋ]

a. 동요하지 않는, 확고한, 의연한
If you describe a feeling or attitude as unwavering, you mean that it is strong and firm and does not weaken.

picture
[píktʃər]

v. 마음에 그리다, 상상하다; (그림으로) 그리다, 묘사하다; n. 그림, 사진
If you picture something in your mind, you think of it and have such a clear memory or idea of it that you seem to be able to see it.

prop*
[prɑp]

v. 받치다, 기대 세우다, 버티다; n. 지주, 버팀목
If you prop an object on or against something, you support it by putting something underneath it or by resting it somewhere.

pillow
[pílou]

n. 베개; 머리 받침대
A pillow is a rectangular cushion which you rest your head on when you are in bed.

bare
[bɛər]

a. 벌거벗은, 있는 그대로의; 텅 빈
If a part of your body is bare, it is not covered by any clothing.

hem*
[hem]

n. (천·옷의) 옷단, 가장자리; vt. 옷단을 대다; 둘러싸다
A hem on something such as a piece of clothing is an edge that is folded over and stitched down to prevent threads coming loose.

embroider
[embrɔ́idər]

v. 자수하다, 수를 놓다, 장식하다
If something such as clothing or cloth is embroidered with a design, the design is stitched into it.

wispy
[wíspi]

a. 숱이 적은, 성긴, 희미한
If someone has wispy hair, their hair does not grow thickly on their head.

grind**
[graind]

v. 갈다, 찧다, 빻다, 비벼 문지르다
If you grind something into a surface, you press and rub it hard into the surface.

clench*
[klentʃ]

v. (손을) 꽉 쥐다; (이를) 악물다; n. 이를 악물기; 단단히 쥐기
When you clench your fist or your fist clenches, you curl your fingers up tightly, usually because you are very angry.

clutch**
[klʌtʃ]

v. 꽉 잡다, 붙들다, 부여잡다; n. 붙잡음, 움켜쥠
If you clutch at something or clutch something, you hold it tightly, usually because you are afraid or anxious.

imprint[*]
[ímprint]

v. 찍다, 새기다, 각인시키다; n. 누른 자국; 흔적
If a surface is imprinted with a mark or design, that mark or design is printed on the surface or pressed into it.

palm^{**}
[pɑːm]

① n. 손바닥 ② n. 종려나무, 야자나무
The palm of your hand is the inside part.

6.
Is the Weather Good for Fishing?

1. Ellen's parents always said _____ is the most important thing.
   (A) education
   (B) being a good friend
   (C) taking fun vacations
   (D) waking up early

2. Why didn't Mr. Johansen go with the girls to the Henrik's house?
   (A) He was too busy at work to go to Henrik's house.
   (B) He didn't want to leave Copenhagen.
   (C) He didn't have time for a vacation.
   (D) He knew it would be safer if he didn't go.

3. How did Annemarie know that her father was speaking in code on the phone?
   (A) He spoke about coffee and there was no coffee available in Copenhagen.
   (B) He said the girls were going on a trip but he didn't say where they were going.
   (C) He spoke about cigarettes and there were no cigarettes available in Copenhagen.
   (D) He spoke about Sweden and Sweden was not involved in the war.

4. Henrik is a _____.

    (A) fisherman
    (B) lawyer
    (C) ship builder
    (D) soldier

5. On the train, Kirsti told the German soldiers that _____.

    (A) Ellen was Jewish
    (B) her fish boots were better than their leather boots
    (C) it was Ellen's New Year
    (D) she would visit Uncle Henrik

6. How did Mama and the girls get to Henrik's house?

    (A) They took the train and then walked along the road to the house.
    (B) They took a car and then walked through the woods to the house.
    (C) They took the train and then walked through the woods to the house.
    (D) They took a bus and then walked along the road to the house.

7. Kirsti spoke about _____ since she had seen it.

    (A) the German solider's gun
    (B) Ellen's necklace
    (C) the castle
    (D) Henrik's house

1분에 몇 단어를 읽는지 리딩 속도를 측정해보세요.

$$\frac{1,982 \text{ words}}{\text{reading time ( ) sec}} \times 60 = (\qquad) \text{ WPM}$$

✿ *Build Your Vocabulary*

suspicious**
[səspíʃəs]

a. 의심하는, 수상쩍은, 의혹의
If you are suspicious of someone or something, you do not trust them, and are careful when dealing with them.

glance^{책슴}
[glæns]

v. 흘긋 보다, 잠깐 보다; n. 흘긋 봄
If you glance at something or someone, you look at them very quickly and then look away again immediately.

murmur^{책슴}
[mə́:rmər]

v. 중얼거리다; 투덜거리다; n. 중얼거림
If you murmur something, you say it very quietly, so that not many people can hear what you are saying.

bald**
[bɔːld]

a. (머리 등이) 벗어진, 대머리의; vi. 머리가 벗어지다
Someone who is bald has little or no hair on the top of their head.

tentative*
[téntətiv]

a. 머뭇거리는, 주저하는; 잠정적인, 임시의 (tentatively ad. 모호하게)
If someone is tentative, they are cautious and not very confident because they are uncertain or afraid.

ease^{책슴}
[iːz]

v. (통증 등이) 가벼워지다, 편해지다; n. 편함, 안정
If something unpleasant eases or if you ease it, it is reduced in degree, speed, or intensity.

rub**
[rʌb]

v. 비비다, 문지르다; 스치다; n. 문지르기
If you rub a part of your body, you move your hand or fingers backwards and forwards over it while pressing firmly.

chin**
[tʃin]

n. 아래턱, 턱 끝
Your chin is the part of your face that is below your mouth and above your neck.

amaze**
[əméiz]

vt. 깜짝 놀라게 하다 (amazement n. 놀람, 경탄)
If something amazes you, it surprises you very much.

doorway^{책슴}
[dɔ́:rwèi]

n. 문간, 현관, 출입구
A doorway is a space in a wall where a door opens and closes.

questioning^{책슴}
[kwéstʃəniŋ]

a. 따지는, 캐묻는; n. 의문, 질문
If someone has a questioning expression on their face, they look as if they want to know the answer to a question.

suspect**
[səspékt]

v. 의심하다, 혐의를 두다; n. 용의자
If you suspect that something dishonest or unpleasant has been done, you believe that it has probably been done.

seldom***
[séldəm]

ad. 드물게, 좀처럼 …않는
If something seldom happens, it happens only occasionally.

struggle***
[strʌ́gəl]

v. 고심하다, 분투하다, 발버둥치다, 몸부림치다; n. 투쟁, 분투
If you struggle to do something, you try hard to do it, even though other people or things may be making it difficult for you to succeed.

reluctant*
[rilʌ́ktənt]

a. 꺼리는, 마지못해 하는, 주저하는 (reluctantly ad. 마지못해서)
If you are reluctant to do something, you are unwilling to do it and hesitate before doing it, or do it slowly and without enthusiasm.

puzzle***
[pʌ́zl]

v. 어리둥절하게 만들다, 곤혹스럽게 하다, 난처하게 하다
(puzzled a. 당혹스러운, 어리둥절한)
If something puzzles you, you do not understand it and feel confused.

sunrise**
[sʌ́nràiz]

n. 해돋이, 일출
Sunrise is the time in the morning when the sun first appears in the sky.

meadow**
[médou]

n. 목초지, 초원
A meadow is a field which has grass and flowers growing in it.

carton
[káːrtən]

n. 큰 상자, 한 통
A carton is a plastic or cardboard container in which food or drink is sold.

cigarette**
[sìgərét]

n. 담배
Cigarettes are small tubes of paper containing tobacco which people smoke.

make a face***
[ ]

idiom 얼굴을 찌푸리다, 침울한 표정을 짓다
If you make a face, you twist your face to indicate a certain mental or emotional state.

weed**
[wiːd]

n. 잡초; v. 잡초를 없애다
A weed is a wild plant that grows in gardens or fields of crops and prevents the plants that you want from growing properly.

suntan
[sʌ́ntæ̀n]

v. 햇볕에 타다; n. 햇볕에 탐, 그을음
Someone who is suntanned has an attractive brown color from being in the sun.

exclaim***
[ikskléim]

v. 외치다, 소리치다
If you exclaim, you say or shout something suddenly because of surprise, fear and pleasure.

deer**
[diər]

n. [동물] 사슴
A deer is a large wild animal that eats grass and leaves.

tame**
[teim]

a. 유순한, 길든; vt. 길들이다
A tame animal or bird is one that is not afraid of humans.

wriggle*
[rígəl]

v. 꿈틀거리다, 몸부림치다; n. 몸부림침, 꿈틀거림
If you wriggle or wriggle part of your body, you twist and turn with quick movements.

peer^{복습}
[piər]

vi. 자세히 보다, 응시하다
If you peer at something, you look at it very hard.

stroll**
[stroul]

v. 한가롭게 거닐다, 산책하다; n. 산책
If you stroll somewhere, you walk there in a slow, relaxed way.

probe*
[proub]

v. 탐구하다, 면밀히 조사하다
If you probe into something, you ask questions or try to discover facts about it.

distort*
[distɔ́:rt]

vt. (얼굴 등을) 찡그리다, 찌푸리다; 비틀다, 뒤틀다; 왜곡하다, 곡해하다
If someone's face or body distorts or is distorted, it moves into an unnatural and unattractive shape or position.

frighten^{복습}
[fráitn]

v. 놀라게 하다, 섬뜩하게 하다; 기겁하다 (frightened a. 깜짝 놀란, 겁이 난)
If something or someone frightens you, they cause you to suddenly feel afraid, anxious, or nervous.

fascination*
[fæ̀sənéiʃən]

n. 매혹, 매료
Fascination is the state of being greatly interested in or delighted by something.

**one's
heart sink**

idiom 가슴이 철렁 내려앉다; 낙담하다
If someone's heart sinks, they start to feel sad or worried.

chirp**
[tʃə:rp]

v. (즐거운 듯이) 말하다; 짹짹 울다; n. 짹짹 (새 등의 울음소리)
You say that a person chirps when they say something in a cheer-ful, high-pitched voice.

brand-new
[brǽndnjù:]

a. 아주 새로운, 신상품의
A brand-new object is completely new.

chuckle**
[tʃʌ́kl]

vi. 낄낄 웃다; n. 낄낄 웃음
When you chuckle, you laugh quietly.

gaze***
[geiz]

vi. 응시하다, 뚫어지게 보다; n. 응시, 주시
If you gaze at someone or something, you look steadily at them for a long time.

blur^{복습}
[blə:r]

n. 흐림, 침침함; 더러움, 얼룩; v. (광경·의식·눈 등을) 흐리게 하다
A blur is a shape or area which you cannot see clearly because it has no distinct outline or because it is moving very fast.

breezy*
[brí:zi]

a. 산들바람이 부는, 시원한, 상쾌한
When the weather is breezy, there is a fairly strong but pleasant wind blowing.

seagull
[sí:gʌ̀l]

n. 갈매기
A seagull is a common kind of bird with white or grey feathers.

soar**
[sɔ:r]

vi. 높이 치솟다, 날아오르다; n. 높이 날기, 비상
If something such as a bird soars into the air, it goes quickly up into the air.

mourn^{중등}
[mɔːrn]

v. 슬퍼하다, 한탄하다
If you mourn someone who has died or mourn for them, you are very sad that they have died and show your sorrow in the way that you behave.

sprawl^{중등}
[sprɔːl]

v. 퍼져 나가다, 넓은 지역에 걸치다; (팔다리 등을) 쭉 펴다, 큰 대자로 눕다
If you say that a place sprawls, you mean that it covers a large area of land.

massive**
[mǽsiv]

a. 크고 무거운, 육중한, 굳센, 강력한
Something that is massive is very large in size, quantity, or extent.

exasperation
[igzæspəréiʃən]

n. 분통, 격분, 격노
Exasperation is the state of being annoyed and frustrated.

prance*
[præns]

vi. 활보하다, 껑충거리며 다니다
If someone prances around, they walk or move around with exaggerated movements, usually because they want people to look at them and admire them.

skip**
[skip]

v. 뛰어다니다, 깡충깡충 뛰다; 건너뛰다, 생략하다
If you skip along, you move almost as if you are dancing, with a series of little jumps from one foot to the other.

sidewalk^{중등}
[sáidwɔ̀ːk]

n. (포장한) 보도, 인도
A sidewalk is a path with a hard surface by the side of a road.

shrug^{중등}
[ʃrʌg]

v. (양 손바닥을 내보이면서 어깨를) 으쓱하다; n. 으쓱하기
If you shrug, you raise your shoulders to show that you are not interested in something or that you do not know or care about something.

outskirt*
[áutskə̀ːrt]

n. 변두리, 교외
The outskirts of a city or town are the parts of it that are farthest away from its center.

tease^{중등}
[tiːz]

v. 놀리다, 골리다, 괴롭히다; n. 골리기, 놀림
To tease someone means to laugh at them or make jokes about them in order to embarrass, annoy, or upset them.

dirt path
[də̀ːrtpæθ]

n. 울퉁불퉁한 길, 비포장도로
dirt (n. 흙) + path (n. 작은 길, 오솔길)

border^{중등}
[bɔ́ːrdər]

v. 테를 두르다; 접경하다, 인접하다; n. 테두리, 가장자리; 경계
If something is bordered by another thing, the other thing forms a line along the edge of it.

faithful^{중등}
[féiθfəl]

a. 충실한, 성실한
Someone who is faithful to a person, organization, idea, or activity remains firm in their belief in them or support for them.

bend***
[bend]

n. 커브, 굽음, 굽은 곳; v. 구부리다, 굽히다, 숙이다
A bend in a road, pipe, or other long thin object is a curve or angle in it.

wag*
[wæg]

v. (꼬리 등을) 흔들(리)다; n. 흔들기
When a dog wags its tail, it repeatedly waves its tail from side to side.

shift^{수능}
[ʃift]

v. 옮기다, 방향을 바꾸다; n. 변화, 이동; 교대
If you shift something or if it shifts, it moves slightly.

dot**
[dɑt]

v. 여기저기 흩어져 있다, 산재하다; 점을 찍다; n. 점
When things dot a place or an area, they are scattered or spread all over it.

skirt^{수능}
[skəːrt]

v. 언저리를 지나다, 비켜가다; 경계[변두리]에 있다; n. 스커트, 치마; 교외, 변두리
Something that skirts an area is situated around the edge of it.

ruffle^{복습}
[rʌ́fəl]

v. 구기다, 헝클다; (마음을) 흐트러뜨리다
When the wind ruffles something such as the surface of the sea, it causes it to move gently in a wave-like motion.

pasture**
[pǽstʃər]

n. 목장, 목초지
Pasture is land with grass growing on it for farm animals to eat.

clearing*
[klíəriŋ]

n. (삼림) 개척지; 청소
A clearing is a small area in a forest where there are no trees or bushes.

7.
The House by the Sea

1. Why was visiting the ocean special to Ellen?

   (A) She had never seen the ocean before.

   (B) Her father used to be a fisherman.

   (C) She only saw the ocean in the summertime.

   (D) Her mother was afraid of the ocean.

2. Why did Uncle Henrik name his boat, Ingeborg?

   (A) He named it for his grandmother.

   (B) He named it for his sister.

   (C) He named it for the King of Denmark.

   (D) He named it for the ocean.

3. Why were Annemarie and Ellen told to stay away from people?

   (A) Mama thought it might be dangerous to explain who Ellen was.

   (B) The people around Henrik's house were dangerous people.

   (C) Henrik did not get along with his neighbors.

   (D) The girls could be kidnapped by the neighbors.

4. What happened to Ellen's necklace?

   (A) The German soldiers took it.

   (B) Ellen wore it at Henrik's house.

   (C) Annemarie gave it back to Ellen.

   (D) Annemarie hid it in a safe place.

5. Mama teased Henrik about _____.

   (A) being a fisherman

   (B) not being married

   (C) not living in the city

   (D) cooking well

6. What special food would Annemarie have for dinner?

   (A) Fish and potatoes

   (B) Cupcakes and cream

   (C) Applesauce and fish

   (D) Steak and milk

7. Which of the following did Annemarie and Ellen NOT do outside Henrik's house?

   (A) They looked across the water to Sweden.

   (B) They put their feet into the water.

   (C) They ran across the meadow.

   (D) They went onto Henrik's boat.

⚘ *Check Your Reading Speed*

1분에 몇 단어를 읽는지 리딩 속도를 측정해보세요.

$$\frac{1{,}350 \text{ words}}{\text{reading time ( ) sec}} \times 60 = (\quad) \text{ WPM}$$

⚘ *Build Your Vocabulary*

awe
[ɔ:]

n. 경외, 외경심; vt. 경외심을 갖게 하다
Awe is the feeling of respect and amazement that you have when you are faced with something wonderful and often rather frightening.

meadow
[médou]

n. 목초지, 초원
A meadow is a field which has grass and flowers growing in it.

chimney
[tʃímni]

n. 굴뚝
A chimney is a pipe through which smoke goes up into the air, usually through the roof of a building.

crooked**
[krúkid]

a. 구부러진, 비뚤어진; 마음이 비뚤어진, 부정직한
If you describe something as crooked, especially something that is usually straight, you mean that it is bent or twisted.

shutter**
[ʃʌ́tər]

vt. 덧문을 달다; n. 셔터, 덧문
A shuttered window, room, or building has shutters fitted to it.

tilt*
[tilt]

v. 기울(이)다; n. 경사, 기울기
If you tilt an object or it tilts, it moves into a sloping position with one end or side higher than the other.

wispy
[wispi]

a. 숱이 적은, 성긴, 희미한
If someone has wispy hair, their hair does not grow thickly on their head.

straw**
[strɔ:]

n. 짚, 밀짚; 빨대
Straw consists of the dried, yellowish stalks from crops such as wheat or barley.

gnarled
[nɑ:rld]

a. 울퉁불퉁하고 비틀린, 뼈마디가 굵은
A gnarled tree is twisted and strangely shaped because it is old.

speckled
[spékəld]

a. 얼룩덜룩한, 반점이 있는
A speckled surface is covered with small marks, spots, or shapes.

ripe**
[raip]

a. 익은, 여문
Ripe fruit or grain is fully grown and ready to eat.

pounce*
[pauns]

vi. 갑자기 달려들다, 와락 덤벼들다
If someone pounces on you, they come up towards you suddenly and take hold of you.

lick**
[lik]

vt. 핥다; n. 핥기, 한 번 핥음
When people or animals lick something, they move their tongue across its surface.

paw**
[pɔ:]

n. (동물·갈고리 발톱이 있는) 발; v. 앞발로 차다
The paws of an animal such as a cat, dog, or bear are its feet, which have claws for gripping things and soft pads for walking on.

dart*
[dɑːrt]

v. 돌진하다; 던지다, 쏘다; n. 던지는 화살, 다트
If a person or animal darts somewhere, they move there suddenly and quickly.

apparent**
[əpǽrənt]

a. 또렷한, 명백한, 외관상의 (apparently ad. 보아하니, 명백히)
If something is apparent to you, it is clear and obvious to you.

damp**
[dæmp]

a. 축축한; n. 습기
Something that is damp is slightly wet.

flatten*
[flǽtn]

vt. 평평하게 하다, 납작하게 하다
If you flatten something or if it flattens, it becomes flat or flatter.

border複終
[bɔ́:rdər]

v. 접경하다, 인접하다; 테를 두르다; n. 테두리, 가장자리; 경계
If something is bordered by another thing, the other thing forms a line along the edge of it.

harbor複수
[hɑ́:rbər]

n. 항구, 항만
A harbor is an area of the sea at the coast which is partly enclosed by land or strong walls, so that boats can be left there safely.

amaze複終
[əméiz]

vt. 깜짝 놀라게 하다 (amazement n. 놀람, 경탄)
If something amazes you, it surprises you very much.

tiptoe複수
[típtòu]

vi. 발끝으로 걷다, 발돋움하다; n. 발끝
If you tiptoe somewhere, you walk there very quietly without putting your heels on the floor when you walk.

giggle複수
[gígəl]

v. 낄낄 웃다; n. 낄낄 웃음
If someone giggles, they laugh in a childlike way, because they are amused, nervous, or embarrassed.

float***
[flout]

v. 뜨다; 띄우다; n. 뜨는 물건, 부유물
If something or someone is floating in a liquid, they are in the liquid, on or just below the surface, and are being supported by it.

cup***
[kʌp]

vt. (손 등을) 잔 모양으로 만들다, 손을 모아 쥐다; n. 컵, 잔
If you cup something in your hands, you make your hands into a curved dish-like shape and support it or hold it gently.

misty*
[místi]

a. 안개가 짙은, 안개 자욱한
On a misty day, there is a lot of mist in the air.

shoreline
[ʃɔ́:rlàin]

n. 해안선
A shoreline is the edge of a sea, lake, or wide river.

squint複수
[skwint]

v. 곁눈질을 하다, 실눈으로 보다; a. 사시의; 곁눈질하는
If you squint at something, you look at it with your eyes partly closed.

hazy*
[héizi]

a. 흐릿한, 안개 낀
Hazy weather conditions are those in which things are difficult to see, because of light mist, hot air, or dust.

strip⁺⁺
[strip]

n. 좁고 긴 땅; 길고 가느다란 조각; v. 벗다, 벗기다, 떼어내다
A strip of land or water is a long narrow area of it.

bob*
[bɑb]

v. 위아래로 움직이다, 까닥까닥 흔들리다
If something bobs, it moves up and down, like something does when it is floating on water.

ruffle⁺⁺
[rʌ́fəl]

n. 파동, 잔물결; 주름 장식; v. 구기다, 헝클다; (마음을) 흐트러뜨리다
A ruffle is a wave-like motion on the surface of water.

dock⁺⁺
[dɑk]

n. 선창, 부두; v. 부두에 들어가다; (우주선이) 도킹하다
A dock is an enclosed area in a harbor where ships go to be loaded, unloaded, and repaired.

anchor⁺⁺
[ǽŋkər]

v. (배를) 닻으로 고정시키다, 닻을 내리다; 고정시키다; n. 닻
When a boat anchors or when you anchor it, its anchor is dropped into the water in order to make it stay in one place.

wade⁺⁺
[weid]

vi. 헤치며 걷다, 힘들여 걷다
If you wade through something that makes it difficult to walk, usually water or mud, you walk through it.

purr*
[pəːr]

v. (기분 좋은 듯이) 그르렁거리다, 부르릉 하는 소리를 내다; n. 그르렁거리는 소리
When a cat purrs, it makes a low vibrating sound with its throat because it is contented.

stroke⁺⁺
[strouk]

① vt. 쓰다듬다, 어루만지다; n. 쓰다듬기, 달램 ② n. 타격, 일격, 치기
If you stroke someone or something, you move your hand slowly and gently over them.

remind⁺⁺
[rimáind]

vt. 생각나게 하다, 상기시키다, 일깨우다
If someone reminds you of a fact or event that you already know about, they say something which makes you think about it.

fix⁺⁺⁺
[fiks]

vt. (식사 등을) 준비하다; 고치다; 고정시키다
If you fix some food or a drink for someone, you make it or prepare it for them.

well fed
[wèlféd]

a. 잘 먹은, 영양이 충분한, 살찐
If you say that someone is well fed, you mean that they get food well.

leap⁺⁺⁺
[liːp]

v. 껑충 뛰다, 뛰어넘다; n. 뜀, 도약
If you leap, you jump high in the air or jump a long distance.

sprig*
[sprig]

vt. 잔가지 모양의 무늬를 넣다, 작은 가지로 장식하다; n. 잔가지, 어린 가지
A sprig is a small stem with leaves on it which has been picked from a bush or plant, especially so that it can be used in cooking or as a decoration.

necklace⁺⁺
[néklis]

n. 목걸이
A necklace is a piece of jewelry such as a chain or a string of beads which someone, usually a woman, wears round their neck.

quilt
[kwilt]

n. (솜·털·깃털 등을 넣어 만든) 누비이불, 침대 덮개, 퀼트 제품
A quilt is a thin cover filled with feathers or some other warm, soft material, which you put over your blankets when you are in bed.

fade
[feid]

vi. 바래다, 시들다, 희미해지다
When a colored object fades or when the light fades it, it gradually becomes paler.

stitch
[stitʃ]

v. 꿰매다, 바느질하다; n. 한 바늘, 한 땀
If you stitch cloth, you use a needle and thread to join two pieces together or to make a decoration.

pat
[pæt]

v. 톡톡 가볍게 치다, (애정을 담아) 쓰다듬다; n. 쓰다듬기
If you pat something or someone, you tap them lightly, usually with your hand held flat.

tidy
[táidi]

a. (tidier-tidiest) 단정한, 말쑥한, 깔끔한; v. 치우다, 정돈하다
Something that is tidy is neat and is arranged in an organized way.

chore
[tʃɔːr]

n. (pl.) (가정의) 잡일, 허드렛일
Chores are tasks such as cleaning, washing, and ironing that have to be done regularly at home.

extend
[iksténd]

v. 넓어지다, 퍼지다; (손·발 등을) 뻗다, 늘이다
If an object extends from a surface or place, it sticks out from it.

tuck
[tʌk]

v. 밀어 넣다, 쑤셔 넣다; n. 접어 넣은 단
If you tuck something somewhere, you put it there so that it is safe, comfortable, or neat.

overhear
[ðuvərhíər]

vt. (overheard-overheard) (상대방 모르게) 우연히 듣다, 엿듣다
If you overhear someone, you hear what they are saying when they are not talking to you and they do not know that you are listening.

8.
There Has Been a Death

1. What did Henrik raise on his farm?

    (A) He raised chickens and cows.

    (B) He raised crops and cows.

    (C) He raised one dairy cow.

    (D) He raised one goat.

2. Why didn't most people in Denmark have butter?

    (A) The Germans ate most of the dairy cows.

    (B) The German soldiers took the butter from the farmers.

    (C) The Danish people sent the butter to Germany.

    (D) The Danish people were not allowed to have dairy cows.

3. The war seemed like nothing more than a ghost-story to Annemarie when _____.

    (A) Mama joked to Kirsti and Annemarie about the German soldiers taking butter from Henrik

    (B) Mama told Annemarie and Kirsti a story about Great-aunt Birte

    (C) Mama told Annemarie and Kirsti about Henrik fishing in the ocean

    (D) Mama joked with Kirsti and Annemarie about Henrik's dirty house

4. What did Mama do inside Henrik's house when the girls played outside?

    (A) She cooked a large feast for Henrik and the girls.

    (B) She cleaned Henrik's house.

    (C) She washed the windows of the house.

    (D) She fixed the hole Henrik's brown sweater.

5. Annemarie thought, _____ was a strange thing for Henrik to say.

    (A) "Tomorrow will be a day for fishing."

    (B) "We will leave very early in the morning."

    (C) "I will stay on the boat all night."

    (D) "Why do I need a wife, when I have a sister?"

6. Why did Mama move the furniture in the living room?

    (A) She made room for Great-aunt Birte's party that night.

    (B) She washed the furniture and put it outside to dry.

    (C) She made room for Great-aunt Birte's casket.

    (D) She didn't like the way that Henrik arranged the furniture.

7. What made Annemarie quite certain that Great-aunt Birte didn't exist?

    (A) Annemarie had never heard of Great-aunt Birte before.

    (B) She didn't see Great-aunt Birte's casket.

    (C) Kirsti didn't know who Great-aunt Birte was.

    (D) Mama often spoke about Great-aunt Birte in family stories.

1분에 몇 단어를 읽는지 리딩 속도를 측정해보세요.

$$\frac{1{,}464 \text{ words}}{\text{reading time (} \quad \text{) sec}} \times 60 = (\quad) \text{ WPM}$$

☼ *Build Your Vocabulary*

haze*
[heiz]

n. 아지랑이, 엷은 연기; v. 흐릿해지다, 안개가 끼다
If there is a haze of something such as smoke or steam, you cannot see clearly through it.

barn**
[bɑːrn]

n. 헛간, 광
A barn is a building on a farm in which crops or animal food can be kept.

pail**
[peil]

n. 들통, 버킷
A pail is a bucket, usually made of metal or wood.

daybreak**
[déibrèik]

n. 새벽
Daybreak is the time in the morning when light first appears.

kneel복습
[niːl]

vi. 무릎 꿇다
When you kneel, you bend your legs so that your knees are touching the ground.

bowl***
[boul]

n. 사발, 그릇, 공기
A bowl is a round container with a wide uncovered top.

burst복습
[bəːrst]

v. 갑자기 …하다; 파열하다, 터지다; n. 폭발, 파열; 돌발
If you burst out laughing or crying, you suddenly begin laughing or crying loudly.

irritate**
[írətèit]

vt. 짜증나게 하다, 화나게 하다 (irritated a. 짜증난)
If something irritates you, it keeps annoying you.

whisker*
[hwískər]

n. (고양이 · 쥐 등의) 수염; 구레나룻
The whiskers of an animal such as a cat or a mouse are the long stiff hairs that grow near its mouth.

dip**
[dip]

v. 담그다, 적시다; 가라앉다, 내려가다
If you dip something in a liquid, you put it into the liquid for a short time, so that only part of it is covered, and take it out again.

crop***
[krɑp]

n. 농작물, 수확물
A plant such as a grain, fruit or vegetable grown in large amounts.

munch*
[mʌntʃ]

v. 우적우적 먹다
If you munch food, you eat it by chewing it slowly, thoroughly, and rather noisily.

(every) now and then

idiom 가끔, 때때로, 이따금
If you do something every now and then, you do it sometimes, but not very often.

oatmeal*
[óutmìːl]

n. 오트밀 (죽), 빻은 귀리
Oatmeal is a thick sticky food made from oats cooked in water or milk and eaten hot, especially for breakfast.

pitcher**
[pítʃər]

① n. 물 주전자 ② n. 투수, 피처
A pitcher is a jug.

spoon**
[spuːn]

vt. 숟가락으로 뜨다; n. 숟가락, 스푼
If you spoon food into something, you put it there with a spoon.

flowered
[fláuərd]

a. 꽃으로 덮인, 꽃무늬로 장식한
Flowered paper or cloth has a pattern of flowers on it.

relocate*
[riːlóukeit]

v. (주거 · 공장 · 주민 등을) 다시 배치하다, 이전시키다
If people or businesses relocate or if someone relocates them, they move to a different place.

rueful
[rúːfəl]

a. 애처로운, 가엾은 (ruefully ad. 가엾게, 비참하게)
If someone is rueful, they feel or express regret or sorrow in a quiet and gentle way.

march***
[maːrtʃ]

① v. 끌고 가다, 데려 가다; 행진하다, 당당하게 걷다; n. 행진, 행군 ② n. 3월
If you march someone somewhere, you force them to walk there with you, for example by holding their arm tightly.

picture***
[píktʃər]

v. 마음에 그리다, 상상하다; (그림으로) 그리다, 묘사하다; n. 그림, 사진
If you picture something in your mind, you think of it and have such a clear memory or idea of it that you seem to be able to see it.

mound**
[maund]

n. 더미, 무더기; 언덕
A mound of something is a large rounded pile of it.

military***
[mílitèri]

n. 군대, 군인들; a. 군사의, 무력의
The military are the armed forces of a country.

arrest***
[ərést]

n. 체포, 검거, 구속; vt. 체포하다, 저지하다
Arrest is an action of taking or being taken into custody by authority of the law.

dart***
[daːrt]

v. 돌진하다; 던지다, 쏘다; n. 던지는 화살, 다트
If a person or animal darts somewhere, they move there suddenly and quickly.

distract***
[distrǽkt]

vt. (마음 · 주의를) 흐트러뜨리다, 딴 데로 돌리다
If something distracts you or your attention from something, it takes your attention away from it.

windowsill
[wíndousìl]

n. 창턱, 창 아래틀
A windowsill is a shelf along the bottom of a window, either inside or outside a building.

sunlit
[sʌ́nlìt]

a. 햇빛을 받은, 햇볕에 쬐인, 밝은
Sunlit places are brightly lit by the sun.

specter*
[spéktər]

n. 무서운 것; 망령, 유령
You talk about the specter of something unpleasant when you are frightened that it might occur.

grim
[grim]

a. 험상스러운, 무서운; 엄한, 엄격한
If a person or their behavior is grim, they are very serious, usually because they are worried about something.

grin
[grin]

n. 싱긋 웃음; v. (이를 드러내고) 싱긋 웃다, 활짝 웃다
A grin is a broad smile.

brilliant**
[bríljənt]

a. 빛나는, 찬란한; 훌륭한, 멋진
You describe light, or something that reflects light, as brilliant when it shines very brightly.

pasture
[pǽstʃər]

n. 목장, 목초지
Pasture is land with grass growing on it for farm animals to eat.

rough-textured
[rʌftékstʃərd]

a. (직물의) 감촉이 거친
A rough-textured surface is not smooth, and having roughness.

lick
[lik]

n. 핥기, 한 번 핥음; vt. 핥다
When people or animals lick something, they move their tongue across its surface.

palm
[pɑːm]

① n. 손바닥 ② n. 종려나무, 야자나무
The palm of your hand is the inside part.

extend
[iksténd]

v. (손·발 등을) 뻗다, 늘이다; 넓어지다, 퍼지다
If someone extends their hand, they stretch out their arm and hand to shake hands with someone.

timid**
[tímid]

a. 소심한, 자신이 없는 (timidly ad. 소심하게)
If you describe someone's attitudes or actions as timid, you are criticizing them for being too cautious or slow to act.

scamper
[skǽmpər]

vi. 재빨리 달리다, 날쌔게 움직이다
When people or small animals scamper somewhere, they move there quickly with small, light steps.

armful*
[ɑ́ːrmfùl]

n. 한 아름
arm (n. 한 팔) + ful (…에 가득)

crowd
[kraud]

v. 군집하다, 붐비다; n. 군중, 인파
If a group of people crowd a place, there are so many of them there that it is full.

bouquet*
[boukéi]

n. 꽃다발, 부케
A bouquet is a bunch of flowers which is attractively arranged.

tsk-tsk
[tisktisk]

vt. 쯧쯧 혀를 차다, 못마땅해 하다; int. 쯧
'Tsk-tsk' is a written representation of the sound made to show you disapprove of something.

untidy
[ʌntáidi]

a. 단정치 못한, 말끔하지 못한
If you describe something as untidy, you mean that it is not neat or well arranged.

rug^{복습}
[rʌg]

n. (방바닥 · 마루에 까는) 깔개, 융단
A rug is a piece of thick material that you put on a floor.

clothesline
[klóuðzlàin]

n. 빨랫줄
A clothesline is a thin rope on which you hang washing so that it can dry.

beat^{복습}
[bi:t]

v. 치다, 두드리다; 패배시키다, 이기다; (심장, 맥박 등이) 뛰다; n. [음악] 박자; 고동
If you beat someone or something, you hit them very hard.

scatter***
[skǽtər]

v. 흩뿌리다, 뿌리다; 뿔뿔이 흩어지다
If you scatter things over an area, you throw or drop them so that they spread all over the area.

broom**
[bru(:)m]

n. 비, 빗자루
A broom is a kind of brush with a long handle.

air***
[ɛər]

v. (의복 등을) 바람에 쐬다, 환기시키다, 널다; n. 공기
If you air clothing or bedding, you put it somewhere warm to make sure that it is completely dry.

old-fashioned^{복습}
[óuldfǽʃənd]

a. 구식의, 유행에 뒤떨어진
Old-fashioned ideas, customs, or values are the ideas, customs, and values of the past.

rag**
[ræg]

n. 걸레, 넝마
A rag is a piece of old, often torn, cloth used especially for cleaning things.

keep an eye on

idiom …을 감시하다, 주목하다
If you keep an eye on someone or something, you watch them or it carefully.

polish**
[páliʃ]

v. 닦다, 윤내다; n. 광택; 세련
If you polish something, you rub it with a cloth to make it shine.

scold^{복습}
[skould]

v. 꾸짖다, 잔소리하다
If you scold someone, you speak angrily to them because they have done something wrong.

boom^{복습}
[bu:m]

v. 쿵 하고 울리다; 번창하다; n. 쿵 하는 소리; 대유행, 붐
When something such as someone's voice, a cannon, or a big drum booms, it makes a loud, deep sound that lasts for several seconds.

twinkle*
[twíŋkəl]

v. (눈이 기쁨 · 즐거움 등으로) 반짝하고 빛나다; 반짝거리다, 빛나다; n. 반짝거림
If you say that someone's eyes twinkle, you mean that their face expresses good humor or amusement.

leak*
[li:k]

v. 새(게 하)다; n. (물 · 공기 · 빛 등이) 새는 구멍
If a liquid or gas leaks, it comes out of a hole by accident.

faucet
[fɔ́:sit]

n. (수도 · 통의) 물 꼭지, 물 주둥이
A faucet is a device that controls the flow of a liquid or gas from a pipe or container.

mock**
[mɔ(:)k]

a. 가짜의, 모의의; vt. 흉내 내며 놀리다, 조롱하다; n. 조롱, 놀림감
You use mock to describe something which is not real or genuine, but which is intended to be very similar to the real thing.

dismay^{빈출}
[disméi]

n. 낙담, 실망, 경악; vt. 낙담[실망]하게 하다
Dismay is a strong feeling of fear, worry, or sadness that is caused by something unpleasant and unexpected.

attic**
[ǽtik]

n. 다락(방), 지붕밑 방
An attic is a room at the top of a house just below the roof.

moth**
[mɔ(:)θ]

n. 나방
A moth is an insect like a butterfly which usually flies about at night.

sleeve**
[sli:v]

n. (옷의) 소매(자락)
The sleeves of a coat, shirt, or other item of clothing are the parts that cover your arms.

anchor^{빈출}
[ǽŋkər]

n. 닻; v. (배를) 닻으로 고정시키다, 닻을 내리다; 고정시키다
An anchor is a heavy hooked object that is dropped from a boat into the water at the end of a chain in order to make the boat stay in one place.

slap^{빈출}
[slæp]

v. 찰싹 때리다; 털썩[탁] 놓다; n. 찰싹 (때림)
If you slap someone, you hit them with the palm of your hand.

make room

idiom 자리를 내다; 길을 양보하다
If you make room, you rearrange or organize things to create space.

chin^{빈출}
[tʃin]

n. 아래턱, 턱 끝
Your chin is the part of your face that is below your mouth and above your neck.

arch**
[áːrtʃ]

v. 둥글게 굽히다, 아치형이 되다; n. 아치
If you arch a part of your body such as your back or if it arches, you bend it so that it forms a curve.

casket*
[kǽskit]

n. (고급스러운) 관; (귀중품 · 보석을 넣는) 작은 상자
A casket is a coffin.

custom***
[kʌ́stəm]

n. 풍습, 관습
A custom is an activity or a way of behaving which is usual or traditional in a society or a community.

burial**
[bériəl]

n. 매장(식)
A burial is the act or ceremony of putting a dead body into a grave in the ground.

relative^{빈출}
[rélətiv]

n. 친척; a. 상대적인, 관계가 있는
Your relatives are the members of your family.

fascinate* [fǽsənèit]

v. 매혹하다, 반하게 하다; 주의를 끌다 (fascinated a. 매혹된, 마음을 빼앗긴)

If something fascinates you, it interests and delights you so much that your thoughts tend to concentrate on it.

tease^{복습} [tiːz]

n. 놀리는 사람, 골리기; v. 놀리다, 골리다, 괴롭히다

If you refer to someone as a tease, you mean that they like laughing at people or making jokes about them.

grouch [grautʃ]

n. 불평꾼; 잔소리; vi. 투덜대다; 토라지다

A grouch is someone who is always complaining in a bad-tempered way.

colorful** [kʌ́lərfəl]

a. 생기 있는; 색채가 풍부한, 다채로운

A colorful character is a person who behaves in an interesting and amusing way.

9.
Why Are You Lying?

1. Henrik thought Annemarie _____.

    (A) shouldn't know anything about the war

    (B) was too scared of the Germans

    (C) was not a brave person

    (D) could be very brave if the time needed her to be

2. Mama and Henrik lied to Annemarie because
    _____.

    (A) they didn't want Annemarie to tell anybody their secrets

    (B) they thought that Annemarie was too young to know the truth

    (C) they wanted to help Annemarie be brave

    (D) they didn't want Annemarie to be taken away by German soldiers

3. What was the truth about Great-aunt Birte?

    (A) She was not dead. She lived in Copenhagen.

    (B) She was not a real person.

    (C) She was killed by the German soldiers.

    (D) She was inside the casket.

4. According to Henrik, when is the easiest time for a person to be brave?

(A) When the person knows everything.

(B) When the person is with friends and family.

(C) When the person does not know everything.

(D) When the German soldiers asked people questions.

5. The people who came to Henrik's house
_____ .

(A) were friends of Great-aunt Birte

(B) brought food so Mama didn't have to cook

(C) told stories about happier times

(D) didn't talk to each other

6. Why didn't Annemarie tell Ellen the truth about Great-aunt Birte?

(A) It was safer for Ellen to believe that Great-aunt Birte was real.

(B) Annemarie wasn't allowed to speak to Ellen that night.

(C) Annemarie was too sad about the death of Great-aunt Birte.

(D) Annemarie thought it was fun to lie to Ellen.

7. Who did NOT go to the house at night?

(A) Ellen's parents.

(B) Mama

(C) Peter Neilsen

(D) Annemarie's father

1분에 몇 단어를 읽는지 리딩 속도를 측정해보세요.

$$\frac{1,682 \text{ words}}{\text{reading time (} \quad \text{) sec}} \times 60 = (\quad) \text{ WPM}$$

✿ *Build Your Vocabulary*

flee**
[fliː]

vi. (fled-fled) 달아나다, 도망치다; 사라지다
If you flee from something or someone, or flee a person or thing, you escape from them.

wander***
[wándər]

v. 돌아다니다, 방황하다; n. 유랑, 방랑
If you wander in a place, you walk around there in a casual way, often without intending to go in any particular direction.

kneel^{복습}
[niːl]

vi. 무릎 꿇다
When you kneel, you bend your legs so that your knees are touching the ground.

straw^{복습}
[strɔː]

n. 짚, 밀짚; 빨대
Straw consists of the dried, yellowish stalks from crops such as wheat or barley.

tan**
[tæn]

vt. (피부를) 햇볕에 태우다; n. 햇볕에 그을음
If a part of your body tans or if you tan it, your skin becomes darker than usual because you spend a lot of time in the sun.

rhythmic*
[ríðmik]

a. 율동적인; 주기적인 (rhythmically ad. 율동적으로)
A rhythmic movement or sound is repeated at regular intervals, forming a regular pattern or beat.

urge***
[əːrdʒ]

v. 촉구하다, 충고하다, 몰아대다, 재촉하다; n. (강한) 충동
If you urge someone to do something, you try hard to persuade them to do it.

spotless*
[spátlis]

a. 더럽혀지지 않은, 오점이 없는
spot (n. 얼룩, 반점) + less (a. …없는)

bucket**
[bʌ́kit]

n. 양동이, 버킷
A bucket is a round metal or plastic container with a handle attached to its sides.

alert**
[ələ́ːrt]

a. 경계하는, 방심하지 않는; n. 경보, 경계; v. 경고하다 (alertly ad. 경계하며)
If you are alert, you are paying full attention to things around you and are able to deal with anything that might happen.

poise*
[pɔiz]

vt. (어떤 자세를) 취하다; 균형 잡히게 하다; n. 균형, 평형
If you poise, you hold something steady in a particular position, especially above something else.

wrinkle^{복습}
[ríŋkəl]

v. 주름이 지게 하다, 구겨지다; n. 주름, 잔주름
When you wrinkle your nose or forehead, or when it wrinkles, you tighten the muscles in your face so that the skin folds.

adjust^{복습}
[ədʒʌ́st]

v. 조정[조절]하다; (옷매무새 등을) 바로 하다; 적응하다
If you adjust something If you adjust what you are wearing, you move it slightly so that it is neater or more comfortable.

false teeth
[fɔ́ːlstíːθ]

n. 틀니, 의치
False teeth is a set of artificial teeth used by somebody who has lost their natural teeth.

splintery
[splíntəri]

a. 쪼개지기 쉬운, 파편의, 파편 같은
Something that is splintery resembles or consists long slender fragments of wood having sharp points.

rattle**
[rǽtl]

v. 왈각달각 소리 나다; 덜걱덜걱 움직이다; n. 덜거덕거리는 소리
When something rattles or when you rattle it, it makes short sharp knocking sounds because it is being shaken or it keeps hitting against something hard.

glance^{복습}
[glæns]

v. 흘긋 보다, 잠깐 보다; n. 흘긋 봄
If you glance at something or someone, you look at them very quickly and then look away again immediately.

pinkish
[píŋkiʃ]

a. 핑크색[연분홍색]을 띤
Something pinkish is in the color between red and white.

sunset**
[sʌ́nsèt]

n. 일몰, 저녁노을
Sunset is the time in the evening when the sun disappears out of sight from the sky.

irregular**
[irégjələr]

a. 불규칙한, 고르지 못한
Something that is irregular is not smooth or straight, or does not form a regular pattern.

stack*
[stæk]

v. 쌓다, 쌓아올리다; n. 더미; 많음, 다량
If you stack a number of things, you arrange them in neat piles.

hay**
[hei]

n. 건초, 건초용 풀
Hay is grass which has been cut and dried so that it can be used to feed animals.

fleck
[flek]

n. 작은 조각, 부스러기; 반점, 주근깨
Flecks are small marks on a surface, or objects that look like small marks.

float^{복습}
[flout]

v. 뜨다; 띄우다; n. 뜨는 물건, 부유물
Something that floats in or through the air hangs in it or moves slowly and gently through it.

deft
[deft]

a. 손재주 있는, 솜씨 좋은 (deftly ad. 솜씨 좋게, 교묘히)
A deft action is skilful and often quick.

pulse**
[pʌls]

n. 맥박, 고동; 파동; v. 고동치다, 맥이 뛰다
Your pulse is the regular beating of blood through your body, which you can feel when you touch particular parts of your body.

questioning
[kwéstʃəniŋ]

a. 따지는, 캐묻는; n. 의문, 질문
If someone has a questioning expression on their face, they look as if they want to know the answer to a question.

lessen**
[lésn]

v. 작게 하다, 감하다, 줄이다
If something lessens or you lessen it, it becomes smaller in size, amount, degree, or importance.

tug*
[tʌg]

v. (세게) 당기다, 끌다; 노력[분투]하다; n. 힘껏 당김; 분투, 노력
If you tug something or tug at it, you give it a quick and usually strong pull.

frothy
[frɔ́:θi]

a. 거품투성이의, 거품 같은
A frothy liquid has lots of bubbles on its surface.

udder
[ʌ́dər]

n. (소 · 양 · 염소 등의) 젖통
A cow's udder is the organ that hangs below its body and produces milk.

damp
[dæmp]

a. 축축한; n. 습기
Something that is damp is slightly wet.

shelf**
[ʃelf]

n. 선반
A shelf is a flat piece which is attached to a wall or to the sides of a cupboard for keeping things on.

rub
[rʌb]

v. 비비다, 문지르다; 스치다; n. 문지르기
If you rub a part of your body, you move your hand or fingers backwards and forwards over it while pressing firmly.

affectionate**
[əfékʃənit]

a. 다정한, 애정 어린 (affectionately ad. 애정을 담고)
If you are affectionate, you show your love or fondness for another person in the way that you behave towards them.

startle
[stɑ́:rtl]

v. 깜짝 놀라게 하다; 움찔하다; n. 깜짝 놀람 (startled a. 놀란)
If something sudden and unexpected startles you, it surprises and frightens you slightly.

dismay
[disméi]

vt. 실망[낙담]당황하게 하다; n. 낙담, 실망, 경악
If you are dismayed by something, it makes you feel afraid, worried, or sad.

confess
[kənfés]

v. 자백하다, 고백하다, 인정하다
If someone confesses to doing something wrong, they admit that they did it.

grasp**
[græsp]

v. 붙잡다, 움켜쥐다; n. 움켜잡기
If you grasp something, you take it in your hand and hold it very firmly.

cock***
[kɑk]

v. 위로 치올리다, (귀 · 꽁지를) 쫑긋 세우다; n. 수탉
If you cock a part of your body in a particular direction, you lift it or point it in that direction.

frighten
[fráitn]

v. 놀라게 하다, 섬뜩하게 하다; 기겁하다 (frightened a. 깜짝 놀란, 겁이 난)
If something or someone frightens you, they cause you to suddenly feel afraid, anxious, or nervous.

determined^{복습}
[ditə́:rmind]

a. 결연한, 굳게 결심한
If you are determined to do something, you have made a firm decision to do it and will not let anything stop you.

frown^{복습}
[fraun]

vi. 얼굴을 찡그리다, 눈살을 찌푸리다; n. 찌푸린 얼굴
When someone frowns, their eyebrows become drawn together, because they are annoyed or puzzled.

bravery**
[bréivəri]

n. 용기, 용맹
Bravery is brave behavior or the quality of being brave.

stiffen**
[stífən]

v. 뻣뻣해지다, 경직되다
If you stiffen, you stop moving and stand or sit with muscles that are suddenly tense, for example because you feel afraid or angry.

hearse
[hə:rs]

n. 영구차; vt. 영구차로 운구하다
A hearse is a large car that carries the coffin at a funeral.

wry*
[rai]

a. 빈정대는, 비꼬는, 풍자적인 (wryly ad. 빈정대면서)
If someone has a wry expression, it shows that they find a bad situation or a change in a situation slightly amusing.

mourn^{복습}
[mɔ:rn]

v. 슬퍼하다, 한탄하다
If you mourn someone who has died or mourn for them, you are very sad that they have died and show your sorrow in the way that you behave.

gleam**
[gli:m]

vi. 빛나다, 반짝이다, 번득이다; n. 번득임, 어스레한 빛
If an object or a surface gleams, it reflects light because it is shiny and clean.

fragile*
[frǽdʒəl]

a. 부서지기[깨지기] 쉬운
Easily damaged, broken or harmed.

papery
[péipəri]

a. 종이 같은, 얇은, 약한
Something that is papery is thin and dry like paper.

flicker*
[flíkər]

v. (등불 · 희망 · 빛 등이) 깜박이다; n. 깜박임
If a light or flame flickers, it shines unsteadily.

solemn^{복습}
[sάləm]

a. 엄숙한, 근엄한
Someone or something that is solemn is very serious rather than cheerful or humorous.

reluctant^{복습}
[rilʌ́ktənt]

a. 꺼리는, 마지못해 하는, 주저하는 (reluctantly ad. 마지못해서)
If you are reluctant to do something, you are unwilling to do it and hesitate before doing it, or do it slowly and without enthusiasm.

stay up^{복습}

phrasal v. 자지 않고 일어나 있다; 그대로 있다
If you stay up, you remain out of bed at a time when most people have gone to bed or at a time when you are normally in bed yourself.

sulk^{복습}
[sʌlk]

vi. 샐쭉해지다, 부루퉁해지다; n. 샐쭉함, 부루퉁함
If you sulk, you are silent and bad-tempered for a while because you are annoyed about something.

trudge
[trʌdʒ]

v. (지쳐서) 터덜터덜 걷다; n. 터덜터덜 걷기
If you trudge somewhere, you walk there slowly and with heavy steps, especially because you are tired or unhappy.

wail
[weil]

n. 울부짖음, 비탄, 통곡; v. 울부짖다, 통곡하다; (큰소리로) 투덜거리다
A wail is a long, loud, high-pitched cry which express sorrow or pain.

nurse***
[nəːrs]

vt. 젖 먹이다; 간호하다; n. 간호사; 유모
When a baby nurses or when its mother nurses it, it feeds by sucking milk from its mother's breast.

infant
[ínfənt]

n. 유아, 갓난아기; a. 유아(용)의
An infant is a baby or very young child.

beard**
[biərd]

n. 턱수염 (bearded a. 수염이 있는, 수염이 난)
A bearded man has a beard.

pray
[prei]

v. 기도하다, 기원하다, 빌다
When people pray, they speak to God in order to give thanks or to ask for his help.

doorway
[dɔ́ːrwèi]

n. 문간, 현관, 출입구
A doorway is a space in a wall where a door opens and closes.

mourner*
[mɔ́ːrnər]

n. 장례식 참석자, 조객; 슬퍼하는 사람
A mourner is a person who attends a funeral, especially as a relative or friend of the dead person.

candlelit
[kǽndlit]

a. 촛불을 켠, 촛불에 비추어진
A candlelit room or table is lit by the light of candles.

gnarled
[naːrld]

a. 울퉁불퉁하고 비틀린, 뼈마디가 굵은
A gnarled tree is twisted and strangely shaped because it is old.

wedge*
[wedʒ]

n. 쐐기[V] 모양(의 물건), 쐐기; vt. 밀어 넣다, 끼워 넣다
A wedge of something such as fruit or cheese is a piece of it that has a thick triangular shape.

cheek
[tʃiːk]

n. 뺨, 볼
Your cheeks are the sides of your face below your eyes.

affection**
[əfékʃən]

n. 애정, 애착, 보살핌, 호의
Your affections are your feelings of love or fondness for someone.

urgency*
[ə́ːrdʒənsi]

n. 긴급, 절박, 위급
Urgency is the quality or state of being urgent.

bare
[bɛər]

a. 벌거벗은, 있는 그대로의; 텅 빈
If a part of your body is bare, it is not covered by any clothing.

dangle*
[dǽŋɡəl]

v. (달랑달랑) 매달(리)다; n. 매달린 것
If something dangles from somewhere or if you dangle it somewhere, it hangs or swings loosely.

10.
Let Us Open the Casket

1. Why did the German soldiers go to Henrik's house?

   (A) They noticed that many people gathered at the house.

   (B) They saw bright lights coming from the house.

   (C) They heard noises coming from the house.

   (D) They saw a casket enter Henrik's house.

2. The soldiers asked _____ about the person who died.

   (A) Annemarie

   (B) Ellen

   (C) Peter

   (D) Mama

3. According to the German soldier, what is the old custom when someone dies?

   (A) Close the casket tightly and not look at the deceased person.

   (B) Pay one's respects by looking at the deceased person's face.

   (C) Put money in the deceased person's casket.

   (D) Kiss the deceased person on the forehead.

4. What did the German soldier do to Annemarie's mother?

    (A) He forced her to open the casket.
    (B) He forced her to kiss Great-aunt Birte on the forehead.
    (C) He pushed her into the casket.
    (D) He slapped her across the face.

5. Mama told the German solider that opening the casket
    _____.

    (A) was dangerous because germs could spread
    (B) was against their customs
    (C) was impossible because the casket was nailed shut
    (D) was a bad idea because she didn't want to see
        Great-aunt Birte's face

6. What helped people relax after the German soldiers left?

    (A) Mama said a prayer.
    (B) Peter closed the dark curtains across the window.
    (C) Mama served people hot tea.
    (D) Peter read from the Old Bible.

7. After Peter finished reading and closed the windows,
    he _____.

    (A) helped Mama
    (B) opened the curtains
    (C) read from a new book
    (D) opened the casket

1분에 몇 단어를 읽는지 리딩 속도를 측정해보세요.

$$\frac{1,294 \text{ words}}{\text{reading time ( ) sec}} \times 60 = (\quad) \text{ WPM}$$

✿ *Build Your Vocabulary*

doorway^{완성}
[dɔ́:rwèi]

n. 문간, 현관, 출입구
A doorway is a space in a wall where a door opens and closes.

elbow**
[élbou]

n. 팔꿈치; vt. 팔꿈치로 쿡 찌르다[떠밀다]
Your elbow is the part of your arm where the upper and lower halves of the arm are joined.

clasp^{완성}
[klæsp]

v. 꼭 쥐다, 악수하다; 고정시키다, 죄다; n. 걸쇠, 버클; 악수, 포옹
If you clasp someone or something, you hold them tightly in your hands or arms.

surge*
[sə:rdʒ]

n. (파도 같은) 쇄도, 돌진; v. 쇄도하다, 밀어닥치다
A surge is a sudden large increase in something that has previously been steady, or has only increased or developed slowly.

bond**
[band]

n. 유대, 인연; 묶는 것, 속박
A bond between people is a strong feeling of friendship, love, or shared beliefs and experiences that unites them.

elderly^{완성}
[éldərli]

a. 나이가 지긋한, 중년이 지난
You use elderly as a polite way of saying that someone is old.

tray**
[trei]

n. 쟁반, 음식 접시; 서류함
A tray is a flat piece of wood, plastic, or metal, which usually has raised edges and which is used for carrying things, especially food and drinks.

(every) now and then^{완성}

idiom 가끔, 때때로, 이따금
If you do something every now and then, you do it sometimes, but not very often.

rocking chair^{완성}
[rákiŋtʃɛ̀ər]

n. 흔들의자
A rocking chair is a chair that is built on two curved pieces of wood so that you can rock yourself backwards and forwards when you are sitting in it.

pad*
[pæd]

vt. …에 덧대다, …에 패드를 대다; n. 덧대는 것, 패드
If you pad something, you put something soft in it or over it in order to make it less hard, to protect it, or to give it a different shape.

doze*
[douz]

v. 꾸벅꾸벅 졸다, 선잠을 자다; n. 졸기
When you doze, you sleep lightly or for a short period, especially during the daytime.

startle ^{복습}
[stάːrtl]

v. 깜짝 놀라게 하다; 움찔하다; n. 깜짝 놀람 (startled a. 놀란)
If something sudden and unexpected startles you, it surprises and frightens you slightly.

sweep ^{복습}
[swiːp]

n. 쓸기, 한 번 휘두름; 청소; v. 휩쓸어 가다, 쓸어내리다
A sweep is a long swinging movement of your arm or a weapon.

sheer**
[ʃiər]

a. 얇은; 순전한, 섞이지 않은; ad. 완전히, 순전히
Sheer material is very thin, light, and delicate.

pull up

phrasal v. (말, 차등이) 서다, 차를 세우다
When a vehicle or driver pulls up, the vehicle slows down and stops.

slam ^{복습}
[slæm]

v. (문 따위를) 탕 닫다, 세게 치다; 털썩 내려놓다; n. 쾅 (하는 소리)
If you slam a door or window or if it slams, it shuts noisily and with great force.

tense ^{복습}
[tens]

v. 긴장하다, 팽팽하게 하다; a. 긴장한, 긴박한; 팽팽한
If you tense your muscles become tight and stiff, often because you are anxious or frightened.

recur*
[rikə́ːr]

vi. 되돌아가다, 회상하다; 재발하다
If something recurs, it happens more than once.

pound ^{복습}
[paund]

① v. 쿵쿵 울리다, 마구 치다, 세게 두드리다; n. 타격 ② n. 파운드(무게의 단위)
③ n. 울타리, 우리
If you pound something or pound on it, you hit it with great force, usually loudly and repeatedly.

gasp**
[gæsp]

v. (놀람 따위로) 숨이 막히다, 헐떡거리다; n. 헐떡거림
When you gasp, you take a short quick breath through your mouth, especially when you are surprised, shocked, or in pain.

weep**
[wiːp]

v. 눈물을 흘리다, 울다
If someone weeps, they cry.

custom ^{복습}
[kʌ́stəm]

n. 풍습, 관습
A custom is an activity or a way of behaving which is usual or traditional in a society or a community.

pay one's respects

idiom …에게 경의를 표하다; …에게 문안드리다
If you pay your respects to someone who has just died, you show your respect or affection for them by coming to see their body or their grave.

gleam ^{복습}
[gliːm]

vi. 빛나다, 반짝이다, 번득이다; n. 번득임, 어스레한 빛
If an object or a surface gleams, it reflects light because it is shiny and clean.

gaze ^{복습}
[geiz]

n. 응시, 주시; vi. 응시하다, 뚫어지게 보다
You can talk about someone's gaze as a way of describing how they are looking at something, especially when they are looking steadily at it.

harsh^頻
[hɑ:rʃ]

a. 거친, 가혹한; (소리 따위가) 귀에 거슬리는 (harshly ad. 거칠게)
Harsh actions or speech are unkind and show no understanding or sympathy.

swallow^頻
[swάlou]

v. 삼키다, 목구멍으로 넘기다; (초조해서) 마른침을 삼키다
If you swallow, you make a movement in your throat as if you are drinking something, often because you are nervous or frightened.

lid^{**}
[lid]

n. 뚜껑
A lid is the top of a box or other container which can be removed or raised when you want to open the container.

condescend[*]
[kàndisénd]

vi. (우월감을 가지고) 베푸는 듯이 대하다; 자기를 낮추다, 겸손하게 굴다
If you say that someone condescends to other people, you are showing your disapproval of the fact that they behave in a way which shows that they think they are superior to other people.

coffin^{**}
[kɔ́:fin]

n. 관(棺); vt. 관에 넣다
A coffin is a box in which a dead body is buried or cremated.

fist^頻
[fist]

n. (쥔) 주먹
Your hand is referred to as your fist when you have bent your fingers in towards the palm in order to hit someone, to make an angry gesture, or to hold something.

rub^頻
[rʌb]

v. 문지르다, 비비다; 스치다; n. 문지르기
If you rub against a surface or rub a part of your body against a surface, you move it backwards and forwards while pressing it against the surface.

polish^頻
[pάliʃ]

v. 닦다, 윤내다; n. 광택; 세련 (polished a. 닦은, 광택 있는)
If you polish something, you rub it with a cloth to make it shine.

stiffen^頻
[stífən]

v. 뻣뻣해지다, 경직되다
If you stiffen, you stop moving and stand or sit with muscles that are suddenly tense, for example because you feel afraid or angry.

chin^頻
[tʃin]

n. 아래턱, 턱 끝
Your chin is the part of your face that is below your mouth and above your neck.

casket^頻
[kǽskit]

n. (고급스러운) 관; (귀중품·보석을 넣는) 작은 상자
A casket is a coffin.

germ[*]
[dʒə:rm]

n. 세균, 병(원)균
A germ is a very small organism that causes disease.

linger^頻
[líŋɡər]

vi. 오래 머무르다, 떠나지 못하다
When something lingers, it continues to exist for a long time, often much longer than expected.

longing^{**}
[lɔ́(:)ŋiŋ]

a. 갈망하는, 동경하는; n. 갈망, 열망
If you feel longing or a longing for something, you have a rather sad feeling because you want it very much.

swift^頻
[swift]

a. 빠른, 신속한
A swift event or process happens very quickly or without delay.

slap^{복습}
[slæp]

v. 찰싹 때리다; 털썩[턱] 놓다; n. 찰싹 (때림)
If you slap someone, you hit them with the palm of your hand.

stagger^{**}
[stǽgər]

v. 비틀거리다, 휘청거리다; n. 비틀거림
If you stagger, you walk very unsteadily, for example because you are ill or drunk.

cheek^{복습}
[tʃiːk]

n. 뺨, 볼
Your cheeks are the sides of your face below your eyes.

spit^{**}
[spit]

v. (spat-spat) 내뱉듯이 말하다; (침 등을) 뱉다; n. 침
If someone spits an insult or comment, they say it in an angry or hostile way.

thumb^{복습}
[θʌm]

n. 엄지손가락; v. (책을) 엄지손가락으로 넘기다
Your thumb is the short thick part on the side of your hand next to your four fingers.

flame^{***}
[fleim]

n. 불꽃, 화염; v. 타오르다; 발끈 화를 내다
A flame is a hot bright stream of burning gas that comes from something that is burning.

spatter[*]
[spǽtər]

v. (액체 방울 등이) 흩어지다, 튀(기)다; n. 튐, 튀기는 소리
If a liquid spatters a surface or you spatter a liquid over a surface, drops of the liquid fall on an area of the surface.

stride^{**}
[straid]

v. (strode-stridden) 성큼성큼 걷다; n. 큰 걸음, 활보
If you stride somewhere, you walk there with quick, long steps.

motionless^{복습}
[móuʃənlis]

a. 움직이지 않는, 부동의, 정지한
Someone or something that is motionless is not moving at all.

relight
[rìːláit]

vt. (relighted-relit) ···에 다시 점화하다
re ('다시'를 뜻하는 접두어) + light (v. 불을 붙이다)

extinguish^{**}
[ikstíŋgwiʃ]

vt. (불·빛 등을) 끄다, 진화하다; 소멸시키다
If you extinguish a fire or a light, you stop it burning or shining.

praise^{***}
[preiz]

vt. 칭찬하다; n. 칭찬
If you praise someone or something, you express approval for their achievements or qualities.

scatter^{복습}
[skǽtər]

v. 뿔뿔이 흩어지다; 흩뿌리다, 뿌리다
If a group of people scatter or if you scatter them, they suddenly separate and move in different directions.

heal^{**}
[hiːl]

v. (상처·아픔·고장 등을) 고치다, 낫게 하다
When something heals it, it becomes healthy and normal again.

bind^{**}
[baind]

v. 묶다, 둘러 감다; 의무를 지우다, 속박하다
If you bind up someone's wound, you tie up a long thin piece of material around their wound in way to protect it.

wound^{**}
[wuːnd]

n. 상처, 부상, 상해; vt. 상처를 입히다
A wound is damage to part of your body, especially a cut or a hole in your flesh, which is caused by a gun, knife, or other weapon.

gradual**
[grǽdʒuəl]

a. 점진적인, 단계적인 (gradually ad. 점진적으로)
Happening or changing slowly over a long period of time or distance.

breeze^{복습}
[briːz]

n. 산들바람, 미풍; vi. 산들산들 불다
A breeze is a gentle wind.

speckled^{복습}
[spékəld]

a. 얼룩덜룩한, 반점이 있는
A speckled surface is covered with small marks, spots, or shapes.

cruel**
[krúːəl]

a. 잔혹한, 잔인한, 무자비한
A situation or event that is cruel is very harsh and causes people distress.

11.
Will We See You Again Soon, Peter?

1. What was inside the casket?

    (A) Apples, cheese, and bread

    (B) Old rags

    (C) Old clothing and blankets

    (D) Towels and blankets

2. How was the jacket given to Ellen different than the clothes she usually wore?

    (A) Ellen only wore clothing from the best stores.

    (B) A tailor always made Ellen new clothing.

    (C) Ellen's mother always made Ellen nice clothing.

    (D) Ellen usually wore dull clothing.

3. How did the baby stay warm?

    (A) Peter gave the baby a sweater from the casket.

    (B) Mama gave the baby Kirsti's sweater.

    (C) Annemarie gave the baby her favorite sweater.

    (D) Mama found a baby sweater inside the casket.

4. What did Peter do to the baby?

    (A) He wrapped the baby in an old sweater.

    (B) He put the sweater over the baby's face.

    (C) He put liquid into the baby's mouth.

    (D) He fed the baby a bottle of milk.

5. Peter gave _____ to Mr. Rosen.

    (A) a packet for Henrik

    (B) food for Henrik

    (C) a package for the German soldiers

    (D) an envelope of money

6. Mama gave _____ to each person in the living room.

    (A) a sweater

    (B) a package of food

    (C) a blanket

    (D) a brown packet

7. The Rosens were going _____.

    (A) to ride in Henrik's boat to Sweden

    (B) to walk through the woods to Sweden

    (C) back to Copenhagen

    (D) to live on Henrik's boat

1분에 몇 단어를 읽는지 리딩 속도를 측정해보세요.

$$\frac{1,411 \text{ words}}{\text{reading time ( ) sec}} \times 60 = (\quad) \text{ WPM}$$

✿ *Build Your Vocabulary*

blink[*]
[bliŋk]

v. 눈을 깜박거리다; (등불 · 별 등이) 깜박이다; n. 깜박거림
When you blink or when you blink your eyes, you shut your eyes and very quickly open them again.

peer[등급]
[piər]

vi. 응시하다, 자세히 보다
If you peer at something, you look at it very hard.

stuff[등급]
[stʌf]

vt. 채워 넣다, 속을 채우다; n. 물건, 물질 (stuffed a. 속을 채운)
If you stuff a container or space with something, you fill it with something or with a quantity of things until it is full.

article[***]
[ɑ́ːrtikl]

n. 물품; 기사, 논설; 조항
You can refer to objects as articles of some kind.

distribute[**]
[distríbjuːt]

v. 분배하다, 배포하다, 배급하다
If you distribute things, you hand them or deliver them to a number of people.

beard[등급]
[biərd]

n. 턱수염
A man's beard is the hair that grows on his chin and cheeks.

murmur[등급]
[mə́ːrmər]

v. 중얼거리다; 투덜거리다; n. 중얼거림
If you murmur something, you say it very quietly, so that not many people can hear what you are saying.

woolen[**]
[wúlən]

a. 양모의, 모직의
Made of the hair that grows on sheep and on some other animals.

rummage
[rʌ́midʒ]

v. 뒤지다, 샅샅이 찾다; n. 잡동사니; 뒤지기
If you rummage through something, you search for something you want by moving things around in a careless or hurried way.

patch[**]
[pætʃ]

v. 헝겊을 대고 깁다; n. 헝겊 조각; 반창고
If you patch something that has a hole in it, you mend it by fastening a patch over the hole.

worn[**]
[wɔːrn]

a. 닳아 해진, 써서 낡은; 지쳐버린, 수척해진
Worn is used to describe something that is damaged or thin because it is old and has been used a lot.

refashion
[riːfǽʃən]

vt. 고쳐 만들다, 개조하다; 꾸밈새를 바꾸다, 모양을 달리하다
re ('다시'를 뜻하는 접두어) + fashion (vt. 만들어내다)

brand-new[복습]
[brǽndnjùː]

a. 아주 새로운, 신상품의
A brand-new object is completely new.

shabby[**]
[ʃǽbi]

a. 초라한, 낡아빠진, 허름한
Shabby things or places look old and in bad condition.

mismatch
[mismǽtʃ]

vt. 잘못 짝을 지우다; n. 부적당한 짝, 어울리지 않는 결혼
To mismatch things or people means to put them together although they do not go together well or are not suitable for each other.

infant[복습]
[ínfənt]

n. 유아, 갓난아기; a. 유아(용)의
An infant is a baby or very young child.

sleeve[복습]
[sliːv]

n. (옷의) 소매(자락)
The sleeves of a coat, shirt, or other item of clothing are the parts that cover your arms.

encase
[enkéis]

vt. 싸다, (상자 등에) 넣다
If a person or an object is encased in something, they are completely covered or surrounded by it.

eyelid[*]
[áilìd]

n. 눈꺼풀
Your eyelids are the two pieces of skin which cover your eyes when they are closed.

flutter[**]
[flʌ́tər]

v. (깃발 등이) 펄럭이다, (새 등이) 날갯짓하다; n. 펄럭임
If something thin or light flutters, or if you flutter it, it moves up and down or from side to side with a lot of quick, light movements.

pound[복습]
[paund]

① n. 파운드(무게의 단위) ② v. 쿵쿵 울리다, 마구 치다, 세게 두드리다; n. 타격
③ n. 울타리, 우리
A pound is a unit of weight used mainly in Britain, America, and other countries where English is spoken. One pound is equal to 0.454 kilograms.

plead[복습]
[pliːd]

v. 간청하다, 탄원하다; 변론하다, 변호하다
If you plead with someone to do something, you ask them in an intense, emotional way to do it.

take a chance

idiom 모험을 하다, 위험을 무릅쓰고 시도하다
When you take a chance, you try to do something although there is a large risk of danger or failure.

insert[**]
[insə́ːrt]

vt. 끼워 넣다, 삽입하다, 넣다
If you insert an object into something, you put the object inside it.

dropper
[drápər]

n. (안약 등의) 액체를 떨어뜨리는 기구
A dropper is a small glass tube with a hollow rubber part on one end which you use for drawing up and dropping small amounts of liquid.

squeeze[**]
[skwiːz]

vt. 꽉 쥐다, 짜다, 압착하다; 쑤셔 넣다; n. 압착, 짜냄
If you squeeze something, you press it firmly, usually with your hands.

yawn [완성]
[jɔ:n]

vi. 하품하다; n. 하품
If you yawn, you open your mouth very wide and breathe in more air than usual, often when you are tired or when you are not interested in something.

swallow [완성]
[swálou]

v. 삼키다, 목구멍으로 넘기다; (초조해서) 마른침을 삼키다
If you swallow something, you cause it to go from your mouth down into your stomach.

grip [완성]
[grip]

v. 꽉 잡다, 움켜잡다; n. 잡음, 붙듦, 움켜쥠; 손잡이
If you grip something, you take hold of it with your hand and continue to hold it firmly.

coffin [완성]
[kɔ́:fin]

n. 관(棺); vt. 관에 넣다
A coffin is a box in which a dead body is buried or cremated.

packet*
[pǽkit]

n. 소포; 한 묶음, 한 다발
A packet is a small flat parcel.

assemble*
[əsémbəl]

v. 모이다, 집합하다; 모으다, 조립하다
When people assemble or when someone assembles them, they come together in a group, usually for a particular purpose such as a meeting.

bulky*
[bʌ́lki]

a. 두꺼운; 부피가 큰
Something that is bulky is large and heavy. Bulky things are often difficult to move or deal with.

overhear [완성]
[òuvərhíər]

vt. 엿듣다, (상대방 모르게) 우연히 듣다
If you overhear someone, you hear what they are saying when they are not talking to you and they do not know that you are listening.

harbor [완성]
[hɑ́:rbər]

n. 항구, 항만
A harbor is an area of the sea at the coast which is partly enclosed by land or strong walls, so that boats can be left there safely.

protrude*
[proutrú:d]

v. 튀어나오다, 비어져 나오다; 내밀다, 내뻗다
If something protrudes from somewhere, it sticks out.

puzzle [완성]
[pʌ́zl]

v. 어리둥절하게 만들다, 곤혹스럽게 하다, 난처하게 하다
(puzzled a. 당혹스러운, 어리둥절한)
If something puzzles you, you do not understand it and feel confused.

contain [완성]
[kəntéin]

vt. 담고 있다, 포함하다; 억누르다, 참다
If something such as a box, bag, room, or place contains things, those things are inside it.

merriment*
[mérimənt]

n. 명랑함, 흥겹게 떠듦
Merriment means laughter.

engagement [완성]
[engéidʒmənt]

n. 약혼; 약속, 계약
An engagement is an agreement that two people have made with each other to get married.

occasional[초급]
[əkéiʒənəl]

a. 가끔의, 때때로의 (occasionally ad. 때때로, 가끔)
Occasional means happening sometimes, but not regularly or often.

instruction[**]
[instrʌ́kʃən]

n. 지시, 훈령; 교육, 교훈
An instruction is something that someone tells you to do.

lighthearted[초급]
[láithá:rtid]

a. 근심 걱정 없는, 마음 편한; 쾌활한, 명랑한
Someone who is lighthearted is cheerful and happy.

grasp[초급]
[græsp]

n. 움켜잡기; v. 붙잡다, 움켜쥐다
A grasp is a very firm hold or grip.

wordless[*]
[wə́:rdlis]

a. 말없는, 무언의; 말로 표현할 수 없는 (wordlessly ad. 말없이)
You say that someone is wordless when they do not say anything, especially at a time when they are expected to say something.

Godspeed
[gádspí:d]

n. 성공[행운]의 축복[기원]
The term Godspeed is sometimes used in order to wish someone success and safety, especially if they are about to go on a long and dangerous journey.

commotion[*]
[kəmóuʃən]

n. 소동, 소요, 동요
A commotion is a lot of noise, confusion, and excitement.

stumble[초급]
[stʌ́mbəl]

v. 발부리가 걸리다, 비틀거리며 걷다; n. 비틀거림
If you stumble, you put your foot down awkwardly while you are walking or running and nearly fall over.

misshapen
[mìsʃéipən]

a. 보기 흉한, 모양이 정상이 아닌
If you describe something as misshapen, you think that it does not have a normal or natural shape.

ill-fitting
[ilfítiŋ]

a. (크기나 모양이) 맞지 않는
An ill-fitting piece of clothing does not fit the person who is wearing it properly.

ragged[**]
[rǽgid]

a. (옷 등이) 찢어진, 해어진; 남루한, 초라한
Ragged clothes are old and torn.

drawn[초급]
[drɔ:n]

a. 찡그린, 일그러진; DRAW(v. 그리다; 빼다, 당기다)의 과거분사
If someone or their face looks drawn, their face is thin and they look very tired, ill, worried, or unhappy.

neat[**]
[ni:t]

a. 산뜻한, 깔끔한 (neatly ad. 깔끔하게)
A neat place, thing, or person is tidy and smart, and has everything in the correct place.

comb[**]
[koum]

v. (머리카락·동물의 털 따위를) 빗질하다, 빗다; n. 빗
When you comb your hair, you tidy it using a comb.

ancient[초급]
[éinʃənt]

a. 옛날의, 고대의
Ancient means very old, or having existed for a long time.

adjust[초급]
[ədʒʌ́st]

v. (옷매무새 등을) 바로 하다; 조절하다, 조정하다; 적응하다
If you adjust something such as your clothing or a machine, you correct or alter its position or setting.

good-natured**
[gúdnéitʃərd]

a. 친절한, 사람이 좋은 (good-naturedly ad. 친절하게)
A good-natured person or animal is naturally friendly and does not get angry easily.

lack***
[læk]

n. 부족; v. …이 없다, …이 결핍되다
If there is a lack of something, there is not enough of it or it does not exist at all.

decent**
[díːsənt]

a. 적당한, 괜찮은, 품위 있는
Decent is used to describe something which is considered to be of an acceptable standard or quality.

daydream*
[déidrìːm]

n. 백일몽, 공상
A daydream is a series of pleasant thoughts, usually about things that you would like to happen.

width**
[widθ]

n. 너비, 폭; 가로
The width of something is the distance it measures from one side or edge to the other.

depth**
[depθ]

n. 깊이; 깊은 곳, 깊음
The depth of something such as a river or hole is the distance downwards from its top surface, or between its upper and lower surfaces.

12.
Where Was Mama?

1. What was NOT true about the walk to Henrik's boat?

    (A) The path was uneven.

    (B) The sunrise helped the Rosens see the path.

    (C) The Rosens didn't know the path.

    (D) It was cold outside and there was no moon in the sky.

2. After the Rosens left the house, Annemarie _____.

    (A) made some food

    (B) looked for her mother

    (C) slept next to Kirsti

    (D) cried

3. While Mama helped the Rosens on the path, Annemarie's father _____ in Copenhagen.

    (A) bought a newspaper

    (B) went to the store

    (C) stayed awake

    (D) went to work

4. Before Annemarie slept, she expected her mom to be home in _____.

   (A) thirty minutes
   (B) one hour
   (C) two hours
   (D) the morning

5. What woke Annemarie?

   (A) Her sister's crying
   (B) The clock in the hall
   (C) A strange noise
   (D) The light from outside

6. When Annemarie woke up, she looked for Mama in
   _____.

   (A) the bathroom
   (B) the room Kirsti and Mama were sharing
   (C) the barn
   (D) the kitchen

7. Where did Annemarie see the moving shape?

   (A) Right outside the door
   (B) At the beginning of the path
   (C) At Henrik's boat
   (D) Under a large tree

1분에 몇 단어를 읽는지 리딩 속도를 측정해보세요.

$$\frac{1{,}131 \text{ words}}{\text{reading time (} \quad \text{) sec}} \times 60 = (\quad) \text{ WPM}$$

✿ *Build Your Vocabulary*

trip***
[trip]

v. 걸려 넘어지다; 경쾌한 걸음걸이로 걷다; n. 여행
If you trip when you are walking, you knock your foot against something and fall or nearly fall.

grasp^{제습}
[græsp]

v. 붙잡다, 움켜쥐다; n. 움켜잡기
If you grasp something, you take it in your hand and hold it very firmly.

regain*
[rigéin]

vt. (잃은 것을) 되찾다, 회복하다
If you regain something that you have lost, you get it back again.

bundle**
[bʌ́ndl]

n. 묶음, 꾸러미
A bundle of things is a number of them that are tied together or wrapped in a cloth or bag so that they can be carried or stored.

stumble^{제습}
[stʌ́mbəl]

v. 발부리가 걸리다, 비틀거리며 걷다; n. 비틀거림
If you stumble, you put your foot down awkwardly while you are walking or running and nearly fall over.

root***
[ru:t]

n. 뿌리, 근원; v. 뿌리박게 하다, 정착하다
The roots of a plant are the parts of it that grow under the ground.

uneven*
[ʌníːvən]

a. 평탄하지 않은
An uneven surface or edge is not smooth, flat, or straight.

breeze^{제습}
[bri:z]

n. 산들바람, 미풍; vi. 산들산들 불다
A breeze is a gentle wind.

meadow^{제습}
[médou]

n. 목초지, 초원
A meadow is a field which has grass and flowers growing in it.

constant***
[kánstənt]

a. 끊임없는; 일정한, 불변의
Happening all the time or repeatedly.

barn^{제습}
[ba:rn]

n. 헛간, 광
A barn is a building on a farm in which crops or animal food can be kept.

dot^{제습}
[dat]

v. 여기저기 흩어져 있다, 산재하다; 점을 찍다; n. 점
When things dot a place or an area, they are scattered or spread all over it.

shiver^{복습}
[ʃívər]

v. (추위 · 공포로) 후들후들 떨다; 전율하다; n. 떨림, 전율
When you shiver, your body shakes slightly because you are cold or frightened.

murmur^{복습}
[mə́:rmər]

v. 중얼거리다; 투덜거리다; n. 중얼거림
If you murmur something, you say it very quietly, so that not many people can hear what you are saying.

fierce^{복습}
[fiərs]

a. 격렬한, 지독한; 사나운 (fiercely ad. 맹렬하게)
Fierce conditions are very intense, great, or strong.

lid^{복습}
[lid]

n. 뚜껑
A lid is the top of a box or other container which can be removed or raised when you want to open the container.

casket^{복습}
[kǽskit]

n. (고급스러운) 관; (귀중품 · 보석을 넣는) 작은 상자
A casket is a coffin.

rocker
[rákər]

n. 흔들의자, 흔들 목마, 흔들리는 것; (요람 등을) 흔드는 사람
A rocker is a chair that is built on two curved pieces of wood so that you can rock yourself backwards and forwards while you are sitting in it.

trace***
[treis]

vt. 추적하다, 자국을 밟아가다; n. 자국, 자취
If you trace someone or something, you find them after looking for them.

scamper^{복습}
[skǽmpər]

vi. 재빨리 달리다, 날쌔게 움직이다
When people or small animals scamper somewhere, they move there quickly with small, light steps.

gnarled^{복습}
[nɑ:rld]

a. 울퉁불퉁하고 비틀린, 뼈마디가 굵은
A gnarled tree is twisted and strangely shaped because it is old.

(every) now and then^{복습}

idiom 가끔, 때때로, 이따금
If you do something every now and then, you do it sometimes, but not very often.

knot**
[nɑt]

v. 얽히게 하다, 매다; n. 매듭; 나무 마디; (knotted a. 얽힌)
If you knot a piece of string, rope, cloth, or other material, you pass one end or part of it through a loop and pull it tight.

clump*
[klʌmp]

n. 수풀, (관목의) 덤불
A clump of things such as trees or plants is a small group of them growing together.

sure-footed
[ʃúərfútid]

a. 발걸음이 흔들리지 않는, 발을 단단히 디디고 선; 틀림없는
A person or animal that is sure-footed can move easily over steep or uneven ground without falling.

rock**
[rɑk]

① v. (앞뒤 · 좌우로 살살) 흔들다, 움직이다; n. 록 음악; 흔들림, 진동
② n. 바위, 암석
When something rocks or when you rock it, it moves slowly and regularly backwards and forwards or from side to side.

oatmeal[음성] [óutmì:l]

n. 오트밀 (죽), 빻은 귀리
Oatmeal is a thick sticky food made from oats cooked in water or milk and eaten hot, especially for breakfast.

dawn[별별] [dɔ:n]

n. 새벽, 동틀 녘; vi. 나타나기 시작하다; 날이 새다, 밝아지다
Dawn is the time of day when light first appears in the sky, just before the sun rises.

creep[별별] [kri:p]

vi. 살금살금 걷다, 기다; n. 포복
If something creeps somewhere, it moves very slowly.

farmland[별] [fá:rmlæ̀nd]

n. 농지, 농토
farm (n. 농장) + land (n. 땅)

blink[음성] [bliŋk]

v. 눈을 깜박거리다; (등불 · 별 등이) 깜박이다; n. 깜박거림
When you blink or when you blink your eyes, you shut your eyes and very quickly open them again.

confusion[별별] [kənfjú:ʒən]

n. 혼동, 혼란, 당황
If your mind is in a state of confusion, you do not know what to believe or what you should do.

horizon[별별] [həráizən]

n. 지평선, 수평선
The horizon is the line in the far distance where the sky seems to meet the land or the sea.

stiff[음성] [stif]

a. 굳은, 뻣뻣한; 완강한, 완고한 (stiffly ad. 뻣뻣하게)
Something that is stiff is firm or does not bend easily.

stretch[별별별] [stretʃ]

v. 잡아 늘이다, 쭉 펴다; n. 뻗침
When you stretch, you put your arms or legs out straight and tighten your muscles.

exhaust[별별] [igzɔ́:st]

vt. 지치게 하다; 다 써버리다, 소진시키다 (exhausted a. 지칠 대로 지친)
If something exhausts you, it makes you so tired, either physically or mentally, that you have no energy left.

journey[별별별] [dʒə́:rni]

n. 여정, 여행
When you make a journey, you travel from one place to another.

quilt[음성] [kwilt]

n. (솜 · 털 · 깃털 등을 넣어 만든) 누비이불, 침대 덮개, 퀼트 제품
A quilt is a thin cover filled with feathers or some other warm, soft material, which you put over your blankets when you are in bed.

crumple[음성] [krʌ́mpl]

v. 구기다, 쭈글쭈글하게 하다; 구겨지다; n. 주름
If you crumple something such as paper or cloth, or if it crumples, it is squashed and becomes full of untidy creases and folds.

cake[별별별] [keik]

v. 들러붙다, 뭉쳐지다; n. 케이크
If something such as blood or mud cakes, it changes from a thick liquid to a dry layer or lump.

barnyard[별] [bá:rnjà:rd]

n. 헛간 앞마당; 농가의 마당
barn (n. 헛간) + yard (n. 마당)

pry
[prai]

① vt. 비틀어 움직이다; 지레로 들어 올리다; n. 지레 ② vi. 엿보다, 동정을 살피다
If you pry something open or pry it away from a surface, you force it open or away from a surface.

purr
[pəːr]

v. (기분 좋은 듯이) 그르렁거리다, 부르릉 하는 소리를 내다; n. 그르렁거리는 소리
When a cat purrs, it makes a low vibrating sound with its throat because it is contented.

fling**
[fliŋ]

vt. (flung-flung) 내던지다, 던지다, (문 등을) 왈칵 열다
If you fling something somewhere, you throw it there using a lot of force.

pillow
[pílou]

n. 베개; 머리 받침대
A pillow is a rectangular cushion which you rest your head on when you are in bed.

overlook**
[òuvərlúk]

vt. 내려다보다; 못 보고 지나치다; 눈감아주다
If a building or window overlooks a place, you can see the place clearly from the building or window.

clearing
[klíəriŋ]

n. (삼림) 개척지; 청소
A clearing is a small area in a forest where there are no trees or bushes.

dim
[dim]

a. 어둑한, 흐릿한, 희미한; v. 어둑하게 하다, 흐려지다
Dim light is not bright.

peer
[piər]

vi. 응시하다, 자세히 보다
If you peer at something, you look at it very hard.

blur
[bləːr]

v. (광경 · 의식 · 눈 등을) 흐리게 하다; n. 흐림, 침침함; 더러움, 얼룩
(blurred a. 흐릿한)
When a thing blurs or when something blurs it, you cannot see it clearly because its edges are no longer distinct.

heap
[hiːp]

n. 더미, 쌓아올린 것; 덩어리
A heap of things is a pile of them, especially a pile arranged in a rather untidy way.

squint
[skwint]

v. 실눈으로 보다, 곁눈질을 하다; a. 사시의; 곁눈질하는
If you squint at something, you look at it with your eyes partly closed.

force
[fɔːrs]

vt. 억지로 …시키다, 강요하다; n. 힘, 폭력, 군사력
If someone forces you to do something, they make you do it even though you do not want to.

13.
Run! As Fast As You Can!

1. How did Mama break her ankle?

    (A) She tripped on the loose step outside of the kitchen.

    (B) She fell on Henrik's boat.

    (C) She tripped on a root.

    (D) She slipped on some wet grass.

2. What did Mama say was the most important thing after Annemarie found her?

    (A) The Rosens were with Henrik.

    (B) Her ankle was not hurt badly.

    (C) Kirsti was safe at home.

    (D) Annemarie found her mother.

3. How did Annemarie's mother get back to Henrik's house?

    (A) She crawled along the path.

    (B) She was driven home by the doctor.

    (C) She walked home along the path.

    (D) One of the neighbors carried her halfway.

4. Mama would tell the doctor that she _____.

    (A) tripped on a root

    (B) fell on the stairs

    (C) helped the Rosens escape

    (D) was kicked by the cow in Henrik's barn

5. What did Annemarie find on the grass at the front of the steps?

    (A) Mr. Rosen's money

    (B) Mr. Rosen's food

    (C) The packet Peter gave to Mr. Rosen

    (D) Ellen's necklace inside a package

6. Annemarie would pretend to take _____ to her uncle.

    (A) lunch

    (B) a package

    (C) a jacket

    (D) fishing supplies

7. Why was it dangerous for Annemarie to go to Henrik's boat?

    (A) German soldiers could stop Annemarie.

    (B) Annemarie could get lost on the path.

    (C) Someone could kidnap Annemarie.

    (D) Annemarie could fall in the water near Henrik's boat.

✿ *Check Your Reading Speed*

1분에 몇 단어를 읽는지 리딩 속도를 측정해보세요.

$$\frac{947 \text{ words}}{\text{reading time (\quad) sec}} \times 60 = (\quad) \text{ WPM}$$

✿ *Build Your Vocabulary*

falter*
[fɔ́ːltər]

vi. 불안정해지다, 흔들리다, 머뭇거리다
If something falters, it loses power or strength in an uneven way, or no longer makes much progress.

dash***
[dæʃ]

v. 돌진하다; 내던지다; n. 소량; 돌격
If you dash somewhere, you run or go there quickly and suddenly.

desperateᴮˢ
[déspərit]

a. 필사적인; 절망적인, 자포자기의 (desperately a. 필사적으로)
If you are desperate, you are in such a bad situation that you are willing to try anything to change it.

kneelᴮˢ
[niːl]

vi. 무릎 꿇다
When you kneel, you bend your legs so that your knees are touching the ground.

winceᴮˢ
[wins]

vi. (아픔·무서움 때문에) 주춤하다, 움츠리다, 움찔하다
If you wince, you suddenly look as if you are suffering because you feel pain.

drawnᴮˢ
[drɔːn]

a. 찡그린, 일그러진; DRAW(v. 그리다; 빼다, 당기다)의 과거분사
If someone or their face looks drawn, their face is thin and they look very tired, ill, worried, or unhappy.

fadeᴮˢ
[feid]

vi. 바래다, 시들다, 희미해지다
When something that you are looking at fades, it slowly becomes less bright or clear until it disappears.

aboard*
[əbɔ́ːrd]

ad. 배에, 승선하여
If you are aboard a ship or plane, you are on it or in it.

cabin***
[kǽbin]

n. 선실, 객실; (통나무) 오두막집
A cabin is a small room in a ship or boat.

anxiousᴮˢ
[ǽŋkʃəs]

a. 걱정하는, 염려하는; 열망하는, 간절히 바라는
If you are anxious, you are nervous or worried about something.

sprawlᴮˢ
[sprɔːl]

v. 큰 대자로 눕다, (팔다리 등을) 쭉 펴다; 퍼져 나가다, 넓은 지역에 걸치다
If you sprawl somewhere, you sit or lie down with your legs and arms spread out in a careless way.

clumsy*
[klʌ́mzi]

a. 서투른, 꼴사나운, 어색한
A clumsy person moves or handles things in a careless, awkward way, often so that things are knocked over or broken.

scold^{복습}
[skould]

v. 꾸짖다, 잔소리하다
If you scold someone, you speak angrily to them because they have done something wrong.

ankle**
[ǽŋkl]

n. 발목
Your ankle is the joint where your foot joins your leg.

mend**
[mend]

v. 고치다; 개선하다; 회복하다 n. 수선, 개량
If a person or a part of their body mends or is mended, they get better after they have been ill or have had an injury.

wry^{복습}
[rai]

a. 빈정대는, 비꼬는, 풍자적인
If someone has a wry expression, it shows that they find a bad situation or a change in a situation slightly amusing.

crawl**
[krɔːl]

vi. 기어가다, 느릿느릿 가다; n. 기어감; 서행
When you crawl, you move forward on your hands and knees.

inch by inch

idiom 조금씩, 차츰
If someone or something moves inch by inch, they move very slowly and carefully.

drunkard*
[drʌ́ŋkərd]

n. 술꾼, 술고래
A drunkard is someone who frequently gets drunk.

faint***
[feint]

a. 희미한, 어렴풋한; vi. 기절하다
A faint sound, color, mark, feeling, or quality has very little strength or intensity.

hobble*
[hάbəl]

vi. 절뚝거리며 걷다
If you hobble, you walk in an awkward way with small steps, for example because your foot is injured.

twig**
[twig]

n. 잔가지, 가는 가지
A twig is a very small thin branch that grows out from a main branch of a tree or bush.

drag***
[dræg]

v. 끌다; 힘들게 움직이다; n. 견인, 끌기
If you drag something, you pull it along the ground.

gaze^{복습}
[geiz]

vi. 응시하다, 뚫어지게 보다; n. 응시, 주시
If you gaze at someone or something, you look steadily at them for a long time.

vast***
[væst]

a. 광대한, 거대한
Something that is vast is extremely large.

border^{복습}
[bɔ́ːrdər]

n. 테두리, 가장자리; 경계; v. 접경하다, 인접하다; 테를 두르다
A border is a strip or band around the edge of something.

stroke^{복습}
[strouk]

① vt. 쓰다듬다, 어루만지다; n. 쓰다듬기, 달램 ② n. 타격, 일격, 치기
If you stroke someone or something, you move your hand slowly and gently over them.

discolor
[diskʌ́lər]

v. 변색시키다; 빛깔이 바래다
If something discolors or if it is discolored by something else, its original color changes, so that it looks unattractive.

swollen**
[swóulən]

a. 부어오른, 부푼
If a part of your body is swollen, it is larger and rounder than normal, usually as a result of injury or illness.

gasp^{복습}
[gæsp]

v. (놀람 따위로) 숨이 막히다, 헐떡거리다; n. 헐떡거림
When you gasp, you take a short quick breath through your mouth, especially when you are surprised, shocked, or in pain.

packet^{복습}
[pǽkit]

n. 소포; 한 묶음, 한 다발
A packet is a small flat parcel.

stricken**
[stríkən]

a. 맞은, 상처받은, 시달리는, 비탄에 잠긴
If a person or place is stricken by something such as an unpleasant feeling, an illness, or a natural disaster, they are severely affected by it.

groan**
[groun]

n. 신음소리; v. 신음하다, 끙끙거리다
A groan is a long, low sound because of pain.

murmur^{복습}
[mə́:rmər]

v. 중얼거리다; 투덜거리다; n. 중얼거림
If you murmur something, you say it very quietly, so that not many people can hear what you are saying.

glance^{복습}
[glæns]

v. 흘긋 보다, 잠깐 보다; n. 흘긋 봄
If you glance at something or someone, you look at them very quickly and then look away again immediately.

pretend^{복습}
[priténd]

v. …인 체하다, 가장하다; a. 가짜의, 꾸민
If you pretend that something is the case, you act in a way that is intended to make people believe that it is the case, although in fact it is not.

empty-headed
[émptihédid]

a. 생각이 없는, 지각없는, 무지한
If you describe someone as empty-headed, you mean that they are not very intelligent and often do silly things.

14.
On the Dark Path

1. What story did Annemarie tell herself on the way to Henrik's boat?

   (A) Little Red Riding-Hood

   (B) Cinderella

   (C) Snow White

   (D) Goldie Locks and the Three Bears

2. Kirsti always _____ when Annemarie told stories.

   (A) yelled out the ending of the story

   (B) asked questions

   (C) interrupted and made up her own story

   (D) asked about the ending of the story

3. Why didn't Annemarie go along the road?

   (A) Someone could see her on the road.

   (B) It was too dark along the road.

   (C) The roads were too busy with fishermen.

   (D) Annemarie enjoyed walking through the woods in the dark.

4. When Annemarie reached the _____, she could start running towards Henrik's boat.

   (A) path
   (B) dock
   (C) road
   (D) meadow

5. Why had Annemarie been to Henrik's boat before?

   (A) She showed Ellen Henrik's boat.
   (B) She walked with Henrik to work in the summertime.
   (C) She used to watch Henrik unload fish in the afternoon.
   (D) She went fishing with Henrik on the weekends.

6. Where was it difficult to see the path?

   (A) Just outside of Henrik's house
   (B) Near the harbor
   (C) In the meadow
   (D) Beside the high blueberry bushes

7. Who did Annemarie see on the path in front of her?

   (A) A pack of wild dogs
   (B) Two German soldiers
   (C) A group of German fishermen
   (D) Four German soldiers with dogs

1분에 몇 단어를 읽는지 리딩 속도를 측정해보세요.

$$\frac{1{,}505 \text{ words}}{\text{reading time (} \quad \text{) sec}} \times 60 = (\qquad) \text{ WPM}$$

☆ *Build Your Vocabulary*

footpath
[fútpæ̀θ]

n. 좁은 길; 보도
A footpath is a path for people to walk on, especially in the country-side.

dawn
[dɔːn]

n. 새벽, 동틀 녘; vi. 나타나기 시작하다; 날이 새다, 밝아지다
Dawn is the time of day when light first appears in the sky, just before the sun rises.

don
[dɔn]

vt. (옷 · 모자 등을) 입다, 쓰다
If you don clothing, you put it on.

peer
[piər]

vi. 응시하다, 자세히 보다
If you peer at something, you look at it very hard.

bulky
[bʌ́lki]

a. 두꺼운; 부피가 큰
Something that is bulky is large and heavy. Bulky things are often difficult to move or deal with.

garment
[gáːrmənt]

n. 의복, 옷; 외피, 외관
A garment is a piece of clothing; used especially in contexts where you are talking about the manufacture or sale of clothes.

chilly
[tʃíli]

a. 차가운, 쌀쌀한; (태도 등이) 냉담한
If you feel chilly, you feel rather cold.

damp
[dæmp]

a. 축축한; n. 습기
Something that is damp is slightly wet.

shiver
[ʃívər]

v. (추위 · 공포로) 후들후들 떨다; 전율하다; n. 떨림, 전율
When you shiver, your body shakes slightly because you are cold or frightened.

clearing
[klíəriŋ]

n. (삼림) 개척지; 청소
A clearing is a small area in a forest where there are no trees or bushes.

outline
[áutlàin]

vt. … 의 윤곽을 그리다; n. 윤곽; 약도
You say that an object is outlined when you can see its general shape because there is light behind it.

underfoot
[ʌ̀ndərfút]

ad. 발밑에, 발치에
You describe something as being underfoot when you are standing or walking on it.

lattice*
[lǽtis]
vt. 격자 구조[무늬]로 하다; 격자를 붙이다
Something that is latticed is decorated with or is in the form of a lattice.

root^{수능}
[ru:t]
n. 뿌리, 근원; v. 뿌리박게 하다; 정착하다
The roots of a plant are the parts of it that grow under the ground.

stumble^{수능}
[stʌmbəl]
v. 발부리가 걸리다, 비틀거리며 걷다; n. 비틀거림
If you stumble, you put your foot down awkwardly while you are walking or running and nearly fall over.

straw^{수능}
[strɔ:]
n. 짚, 밀짚; 빨대
Straw consists of the dried, yellowish stalks from crops such as wheat or barley.

shift^{수능}
[ʃift]
v. 옮기다, 방향을 바꾸다; n. 변화, 이동; 교대
If you shift something or if it shifts, it moves slightly.

cuddle*
[kʌdl]
v. 꼭 껴안다, 껴안고 귀여워하다
If you cuddle someone, you put your arms round them and hold them close as a way of showing your affection.

cloak**
[klouk]
n. 외투, 망토
A cloak is a long, loose, sleeveless piece of clothing which people used to wear over their other clothes when they went out.

hood**
[hud]
n. 두건; 자동차 보닛, 덮개
A hood is a part of a coat which you can pull up to cover your head. It is in the shape of a triangular bag attached to the neck of the coat at the back.

interrupt^{수능}
[ìntərʌpt]
v. 방해하다, 가로막다, 저지하다
If you interrupt someone who is speaking, you say or do something that causes them to stop.

squirrel**
[skwə́:rəl]
n. 다람쥐
A squirrel is a small animal with a long furry tail.

scamper^{수능}
[skǽmpər]
vi. 재빨리 달리다, 날쌔게 움직이다
When people or small animals scamper somewhere, they move there quickly with small, light steps.

frighten^{수능}
[fráitn]
v. 놀라게 하다, 섬뜩하게 하다; 기겁하다 (frightened a. 깜짝 놀란, 겁이 난)
If something or someone frightens you, they cause you to suddenly feel afraid, anxious, or nervous.

beast***
[bi:st]
n. 야수, 짐승; 짐승 같은 인간
You can refer to an animal as a beast, especially if it is a large, dangerous, or unusual one.

populate*
[pápjəlèit]
v. …에 거주하다, 살다; 거주시키다
If an area is populated by certain people or animals, those people or animals live there, often in large numbers.

vivid**
[vívid]
a. 생생한, 발랄한
If you describe memories and descriptions as vivid, you mean that they are very clear and detailed.

snuggle
[snʌ́gəl]

v. 달라붙다; 껴안다, 끌어안다; n. 다가붙음
If you snuggle somewhere, you settle yourself into a warm, comfortable position, especially by moving closer to another person.

widen*
[wáidn]

v. 넓히다; 넓게 되다
If you widen something or if it widens, it becomes greater in measurement from one side or edge to the other.

flatten
[flǽtn]

vt. 평평하게 하다, 납작하게 하다
If you flatten something or if it flattens, it becomes flat or flatter.

hold out

phrasal v. (손 혹은 손에 든 것을) 내밀다, 내뻗다
If you hold out your hand, you move your hand away from your body, for example to shake hands.

wriggle
[rígəl]

v. 꿈틀거리다, 몸부림치다; n. 몸부림침, 꿈틀거림
If you wriggle or wriggle part of your body, you twist and turn with quick movements.

bark
[bɑːrk]

v. 짖다; 고함치다, 소리 지르며 말하다
When a dog barks, it makes a short, loud noise, once or several times.

chase**
[tʃeis]

v. 뒤쫓다; 추구하다; 쫓아내다; n. 추적, 추격
If you chase someone, or chase after them, you run after them or follow them quickly in order to catch or reach them.

churn
[tʃəːrn]

v. (물 · 파도 등이) 마구 휘돌다, 휘젓다; 거품이 나(게 하다); (속이) 뒤틀리다
If something churns water, mud, or dust, it moves it about violently.

segment*
[ségmənt]

n. 부분, 단편, 조각
A segment of something is one part of it, considered separately from the rest.

swollen
[swóulən]

a. 부어오른, 부푼
If a part of your body is swollen, it is larger and rounder than normal, usually as a result of injury or illness.

brusque
[brʌsk]

a. 무뚝뚝한, 퉁명스러운
If you describe a person or their behavior as brusque, you mean that they deal with things, or say things, quickly and shortly, so that they seem to be rude.

businesslike*
[bíznislàik]

a. 사무적인, 업무에 충실한
If you describe someone as businesslike, you mean that they deal with things in an efficient way without wasting time.

battered
[bǽtərd]

a. 오래 써서 낡은; 박살난
Something that is battered is old and in poor condition because it has been used a lot.

dirt road
[də́ːrtroud]

n. 비포장도로
dirt (n. 흙) + road (n. 길, 도로)

wail
[weil]

v. 울부짖다, 통곡하다; (큰소리로) 투덜거리다; n. 울부짖음, 비탄, 통곡
If someone wails, they make long, loud, high-pitched cries which express sorrow or pain.

earache
[íərèik]

n. 귀앓이
Earache is a pain in the inside part of your ear.

grease**
[gri:s]

n. 기름, 지방분; v. …에 기름을 바르다[치다]
Grease is animal fat that is produced by cooking meat.

fork**
[fɔːrk]

n. 갈림길, 포크, 갈퀴; v. 두 갈래 지(게 하)다, 포크 모양으로 하다
A fork in a road, path, or river is a point at which it divides into two parts and forms a 'Y' shape.

harbor^{배출}
[háːrbər]

n. 항구, 항만 (harborside n. 부둣가)
A harbor is an area of the sea at the coast which is partly enclosed by land or strong walls, so that boats can be left there safely.

anchor^{배출}
[ǽŋkər]

n. 닻; v. (배를) 닻으로 고정시키다, 닻을 내리다; 고정시키다
An anchor is a heavy hooked object that is dropped from a boat into the water at the end of a chain in order to make the boat stay in one place.

unload*
[ʌnlóud]

v. (차 · 배 등의) 짐을 내리다; (마음 등의) 짐을 덜다
If you unload goods from a vehicle, or you unload a vehicle, you remove the goods from the vehicle, usually after they have been transported from one place to another.

slippery^{배출}
[slípəri]

a. 미끄러운, 미끈거리는
Something that is slippery is smooth, wet, or oily and is therefore difficult to walk on or to hold.

shimmer*
[ʃímər]

vi. 희미하게 반짝이다, 빛나다; n. 반짝임
If something shimmers, it shines with a faint, unsteady light or has an unclear, unsteady appearance.

herring*
[hériŋ]

n. 청어
A herring is a long silver-colored fish. Herring live in large groups in the sea.

flop*
[flɑp]

v. 퍼덕거리다; 펄썩[털썩] 쓰러지다; n. 펄썩[털썩] 떨어짐
If something flops onto something else, it falls there heavily or untidily.

scent**
[sent]

n. 냄새, 향기; v. 냄새 맡다; 냄새를 풍기다
The scent of a person or animal is the smell that they leave and that other people sometimes follow when looking for them.

sidewalk^{배출}
[sáidwɔ̀ːk]

n. (포장한) 보도, 인도
A sidewalk is a path with a hard surface by the side of a road.

rustle**
[rʌ́səl]

vi. 바스락거리다, 살랑살랑 소리 내다; n. 바스락거리는 소리
If things such as paper or leaves rustle, or if you rustle them, they move about and make a soft, dry sound.

prolong**
[proulɔ́ːŋ]

vt. 늘이다, 연장하다
To prolong something means to make it last longer.

suspense*
[səspéns]

n. 지속적 긴장감, 조마조마한 상태; 미결, 미정
Suspense is a state of excitement or anxiety about something that is going to happen very soon, for example about some news that you are waiting to hear.

tantalize
[tǽntəlàiz]

vt. 감질나게[애타게] 하다
If someone or something tantalizes you, they make you feel hopeful and excited about getting what you want.

dread**
[dred]

n. 공포; 불안; v. 겁내다, 두려워하다; a. 대단히 무서운
Dread is a feeling of great anxiety and fear about something that may happen.

growl**
[graul]

n. 으르렁거리는 소리; v. 으르렁거리다, 고함치다
A growl is a low noise from throat, usually because of anger.

landscape복습
[lǽndskèip]

n. 풍경, 경치
The landscape is everything you can see when you look across an area of land, including hills, rivers, buildings, trees, and plants.

dock복습
[dɑk]

n. 선창, 부두; v. 부두에 들어가다; (우주선이) 도킹하다
A dock is an enclosed area in a harbor where ships go to be loaded, unloaded, and repaired.

gull*
[gʌl]

n. 갈매기
A gull is a common sea bird.

cautious**
[kɔ́ːʃəs]

a. 조심성 있는, 신중한 (cautiously ad. 조심스럽게)
Someone who is cautious acts very carefully in order to avoid possible danger.

strain*
[strein]

v. 잡아당기다, 팽팽하게 하다; 힘껏 작용시키다, 긴장시키다; n. 팽팽함, 긴장
If you strain something, you push, pull, or stretch it in a way that may damage it.

taut
[tɔːt]

a. 팽팽하게 찬; 긴장된
Something that is taut is stretched very tight.

leash
[liːʃ]

n. 가죽 끈, 사슬; 속박, 통제
A dog's leash is a long thin piece of leather or a chain, which you attach to the dog's collar so that you can keep the dog under control.

glitter**
[glítər]

vi. 반짝반짝 빛나다, 반짝이다; n. 반짝이는 작은 장식; 반짝거림, 광채
If something glitters, light comes from or is reflected off different parts of it.

15.
My Dogs Smell Meat!

1. How did Annemarie behave around the German soldiers?

    (A) She was quiet and she didn't answer any questions.

    (B) She acted like Kirsti.

    (C) She was nervous and hardly spoke to the soldiers.

    (D) She made jokes and tried to make the soldiers laugh.

2. What did the dogs do when the soldiers stopped Annemarie?

    (A) They growled at Annemarie and looked into her eyes.

    (B) They looked at the forest behind Annemarie.

    (C) They bit Annemarie's basket.

    (D) They growled and looked at Annemarie's basket.

3. What did the German soldier do with the bread from the basket?

    (A) He threw it on the ground and stepped on it.

    (B) He broke it into pieces and ate it.

    (C) He left it in the basket.

    (D) He fed it to the dogs.

4. The German solider said the dog smelled _____ in the basket.

   (A) meat
   (B) cheese
   (C) blood
   (D) a handkerchief

5. Annemarie started crying when the soldiers

   _____.

   (A) threw the apple on the ground
   (B) asked about the packet
   (C) fed the bread to the dogs
   (D) threw the handkerchief on the ground

6. The German solider called Annemarie's mother stupid because _____.

   (A) she sent Henrik a handkerchief
   (B) she didn't send Henrik any meat with his lunch
   (C) she had better things to do than hemming a handkerchief
   (D) she sent a young girl to give Henrik his lunch

7. Why did Henrik say everything was alright because of Annemarie?

   (A) Annemarie delivered the packet.
   (B) The German dogs would choke on the bread.
   (C) Annemarie spoke with the German soldiers.
   (D) Annemarie gave Henrik cheese and an apple for lunch.

1분에 몇 단어를 읽는지 리딩 속도를 측정해보세요.

$$\frac{1,404 \text{ words}}{\text{reading time } (\quad) \text{ sec}} \times 60 = (\quad) \text{ WPM}$$

✿ *Build Your Vocabulary*

race^{복습}
[reis]

① v. 질주하다, 경주하다, 달리다; ② n. 경주 n. 인종, 민족
If your heart races, it beats very quickly because you are excited or afraid.

pretend^{복습}
[priténd]

v. …인 체하다, 가장하다; a. 가짜의, 꾸민
If you pretend that something is the case, you act in a way that is intended to make people believe that it is the case, although in fact it is not.

amuse^{복습}
[əmjúːz]

vt. 즐겁게 하다, 재미나게 하다
If something amuses you, it makes you want to laugh or smile.

will***
[wil]

v. 의지력을 발휘하다, 애를 쓰다; n. 의지; 유언장
If you will something to happen, you try to make it happen by using mental effort rather than physical effort.

tense^{복습}
[tens]

a. 긴장한, 긴박한; 팽팽한 v. 긴장하다, 팽팽하게 하다
If you are tense, you are anxious and nervous and cannot relax.

alert^{복습}
[əlɔ́ːrt]

a. 경계하는, 방심하지 않는; n. 경보, 경계; v. 경고하다
If you are alert, you are paying full attention to things around you and are able to deal with anything that might happen.

leash^{복습}
[liːʃ]

n. 가죽 끈, 사슬; 속박, 통제
A dog's leash is a long thin piece of leather or a chain, which you attach to the dog's collar so that you can keep the dog under control.

hold out^{복습}

phrasal v. (손 혹은 손에 든 것을) 내밀다, 내뻗다
If you hold out your hand, you move your hand away from your body, for example to shake hands.

loaf**
[louf]

n. (일정한 모양으로 구워 낸 빵의) 덩어리, 빵 한 덩어리
A loaf of bread is bread which has been shaped and baked in one piece.

glance^{복습}
[glæns]

v. 흘긋 보다, 잠깐 보다; n. 흘긋 봄
If you glance at something or someone, you look at them very quickly and then look away again immediately.

scan*
[skæn]

v. 훑어 보다; 자세히 조사하다; 스캔하다; n. 정밀 검사; 스캔
When you scan a place or group of people, you look at it carefully, usually because you are looking for something or someone.

growl^{복습}
[graul]

v. 으르렁거리다, 고함치다; n. 으르렁거리는 소리
When a dog or other animal growls, it makes a low noise in its throat, usually because it is angry.

daybreak^{복습}
[déibrèik]

n. 새벽
Daybreak is the time in the morning when light first appears.

giggle^{복습}
[gígəl]

v. 낄낄 웃다; n. 낄낄 웃음
If someone giggles, they laugh in a childlike way, because they are amused, nervous, or embarrassed.

make a face^{복습}
idiom 얼굴을 찌푸리다, 침울한 표정을 짓다
If you make a face, you twist your face to indicate a certain mental or emotional state.

starve**
[stɑːrv]

v. 굶주리다, 굶어죽다
If people starve, they suffer greatly from lack of food which sometimes leads to their death.

chatter^{복습}
[tʃǽtər]

v. 수다를 떨다, 재잘거리다; 지저귀다
If you chatter, you talk quickly and continuously, usually about things which are not important.

crumb*
[krʌm]

n. 작은 조각, 빵 부스러기, 빵가루
Crumbs are tiny pieces that fall from bread, biscuits, or cake when you cut it or eat it.

crisp**
[krisp]

a. (음식물이) 파삭파삭한, (야채 · 과일 등이) 아삭아삭하는; 상쾌한
Food that is crisp is pleasantly hard, or has a pleasantly hard surface.

fist^{복습}
[fist]

n. (쥔) 주먹
Your hand is referred to as your fist when you have bent your fingers in towards the palm in order to hit someone, to make an angry gesture, or to hold something.

enrage*
[enréidʒ]

vt. 몹시 화나게 하다, 노하게 하다
If you are enraged by something, it makes you extremely angry.

toss**
[tɔːs]

v. 던지다, 내던지다
If you toss something somewhere, you throw it there lightly, often in a rather careless way.

consume**
[kənsúːm]

v. 먹어버리다; 소비하다, 소모하다
If you consume something, you eat or drink it.

snap**
[snæp]

v. 덥석 물다; 홱 잡다, 짤깍 소리 내다; 날카롭게[느닷없이] 말하다; n. 툭 소리 냄
If an animal such as a dog snaps at you, it opens and shuts its jaws quickly near you, as if it were going to bite you.

gulp*
[gʌlp]

v. 꿀꺽꿀꺽 마시다; (긴장, 흥분으로) 침을 꿀꺽 삼키다; n. 꿀꺽꿀꺽 마심
If you gulp something, you eat or drink it very quickly by swallowing large quantities of it at once.

bark^{복습}
[bɑːrk]

v. 고함치다, 소리 지르며 말하다; 짖다
If you bark at someone, you shout at them aggressively in a loud, rough voice.

wedge^{복습}
[wedʒ]

n. 쐐기[V] 모양(의 물건); 쐐기; vt. 밀어 넣다, 끼워 넣다
A wedge of something such as fruit or cheese is a piece of it that has a thick triangular shape.

exasperate^{복습}
[igzǽspərèit]

vt. 성나게 하다, 격분시키다 (exasperated a. 화가 치민, 짜증스러운)
If something exasperates you, they annoy you and make you feel frustrated or upset.

impatient**
[impéiʃənt]

a. 성급한, 조급한, 참을성 없는 (impatiently ad. 성급하게, 조바심 내며)
Easily annoyed by someone's mistakes or because you have to wait.

disgust^{복습}
[disgʌ́st]

n. 혐오감, 싫음; vt. 역겹게 하다, 넌더리나게 하다
Disgust is a feeling of very strong dislike or disapproval.

wither**
[wíðər]

v. 위축시키다, 움츠러들게 하다; 시들다, 말라죽다
(withering a. 위축시키는, 움츠러들게 하는)
A withering look or remark is very critical, and is intended to make someone feel ashamed or stupid.

insolent*
[ínsələnt]

a. 건방진, 오만한, 무례한 (insolently ad. 건방지게)
If you say that someone is being insolent, you mean they are being rude to someone they ought to be respectful to.

implore**
[implɔ́ːr]

vt. 애원하다, 탄원하다
If you implore someone to do something, you ask them to do it in a forceful, emotional way.

bruise**
[bruːz]

v. 멍들게 하다, … 에게 타박상을 주다; n. 타박상, 멍 (bruised a. 멍든)
If a fruit, vegetable, or plant bruises or is bruised, it is damaged by being handled roughly, making a mark on the skin.

sniff^{복습}
[snif]

v. 코를 킁킁거리다, 냄새를 맡다; 콧방귀를 뀌다; n. 냄새 맡음; 콧방귀
If you sniff something or sniff at it, you smell it by breathing air through your nose.

intent**
[intént]

① a. 집중된, 열심인, 여념이 없는 (intently ad. 골똘하게) ② n. 의지, 의향
If someone does something in an intent way, they pay great attention to what they are doing.

saliva
[səláivə]

n. 침, 타액
Saliva is the watery liquid that forms in your mouth and helps you to chew and digest food.

glisten*
[glísn]

vi. 반짝이다, 반짝반짝 빛나다; n. 반짝임
If something glistens, it shines, usually because it is wet or oily.

gum
[gum]

① n. 잇몸, 치은 ② n. 고무질, 점성 고무
Your gums are the areas of firm, pink flesh inside your mouth, which your teeth grow out of.

squirrel^{복습}
[skwə́ːrəl]

n. 다람쥐
A squirrel is a small animal with a long furry tail.

flowered^{복습}
[fláuərd]

a. 꽃으로 덮인, 꽃무늬로 장식한
Flowered paper or cloth has a pattern of flowers on it.

freeze[*][*]
[fri:z]

v. (froze-frozen) 얼다, 얼어붙다; 얼게 하다; n. 결빙
If someone who is moving freezes, they suddenly stop and become completely still and quiet.

scornful[신출]
[skɔ́:rnfəl]

a. 조소하는, 경멸하는, 업신여기는 (scornfully ad. 깔보며, 경멸적으로)
If you are scornful of someone or something, you show contempt for them.

crumple[신출]
[krʌ́mpl]

v. 구기다, 쭈글쭈글하게 하다; 구겨지다; n. 주름
If you crumple something such as paper or cloth, or if it crumples, it is squashed and becomes full of untidy creases and folds.

contempt[신출]
[kəntémpt]

n. 모욕, 경멸
If you have contempt for someone or something, you have no respect for them or think that they are unimportant.

stamp[*][*][*]
[stæmp]

v. (발을) 구르다, 짓밟다; 날인하다; n. 우표, 인지; 도장
If you stamp or stamp your foot, you lift your foot and put it down very hard on the ground, for example because you are angry.

choke[*][*]
[tʃouk]

v. 숨이 막히다, 질식시키다; n. 질식
When you choke or when something chokes you, you cannot breathe properly or get enough air into your lungs.

ruin[*][*][*]
[rú:in]

v. 망치다, 못쓰게 만들다; 몰락하다; n. 파멸, 멸망
To ruin something means to severely harm, damage, or spoil it.

whine[*]
[hwain]

v. 징징거리다, 우는소리를 하다; 푸념하다; n. (탄환·바람 등의) 윙 소리; 흐느낌
If something or someone whines, they make a long, high-pitched noise, especially one which sounds sad or unpleasant.

struggle[신출]
[strʌ́gəl]

v. 고심하다, 분투하다, 발버둥치다, 몸부림치다; n. 투쟁, 분투
If you struggle when you are being held, you twist, kick, and move violently in order to get free.

nose[*][*][*]
[nouz]

v. 코를 비벼대다, 냄새 맡다; n. 코, 후각
If a vehicle noses in a certain direction or if you nose it there, you move it slowly and carefully in that direction.

mutter[*][*]
[mʌ́tər]

v. 중얼거리다, 불평하다; n. 중얼거림, 불평
If you mutter, you speak very quietly so that you cannot easily be heard, often because you are complaining about something.

packet[신출]
[pǽkit]

n. 소포; 한 묶음, 한 다발
A packet is a small flat parcel.

wipe[*][*]
[waip]

vt. 닦다, 닦아 내다; n. 닦음, 닦아 냄
If you wipe something, you rub its surface to remove dirt or liquid from it.

sleeve[신출]
[sli:v]

n. (옷의) 소매(자락)
The sleeves of a coat, shirt, or other item of clothing are the parts that cover your arms.

tear[신출]
[tɛər]

① v. (tore-torn) 찢다, 찢어지다; n. 찢음 ② n. 눈물
If you tear paper, cloth, or another material, or if it tears, you pull it into two pieces or you pull it so that a hole appears in it.

strain^{복습}
[strein]

v. 잡아당기다, 팽팽하게 하다; 긴장시키다; n. 팽팽함, 긴장
If you strain something, you push, pull, or stretch it in a way that may damage it.

snarl[*]
[snɑ:rl]

v. 으르렁거리다, 으르렁거리듯 말하다; n. 으르렁거림
If you snarl something, you say it in a fierce, angry way.

muscle^{**}
[mʌ́səl]

n. 근육
A muscle is a piece of tissue inside your body which connects two bones and which you use when you make a movement.

beneath^{복습}
[biní:θ]

prep. ⋯의 아래[밑]에, ⋯보다 낮은
Something that is beneath another thing is under the other thing.

sleek[*]
[sli:k]

a. 매끄러운, 윤기 나는
Sleek hair or fur is smooth and shiny and looks healthy.

flesh^{***}
[fleʃ]

n. 살, 육체; vt. 살에 찌르다
Flesh is the soft part of a person's or animal's body between the bones and the skin.

glare^{복습}
[glɛər]

v. 노려보다; 번쩍번쩍 빛나다; n. 섬광; 노려봄
If you glare at someone, you look at them with an angry expression on your face.

idiot[*]
[ídiət]

n. 얼간이, 바보
Idiot means stupid.

harsh^{복습}
[hɑ:rʃ]

a. 거친, 가혹한; (소리 따위가) 귀에 거슬리는 (harshly ad. 거칠게)
Harsh actions or speech are unkind and show no understanding or sympathy.

handker-chief^{**}
[hǽŋkərtʃif]

n. 손수건
A handkerchief is a small square piece of fabric which you use for blowing your nose.

hem^{복습}
[hem]

vt. 옷단을 대다; 둘러싸다; n. (천·옷의) 옷단, 가장자리
If you hem something, you form a hem along its edge.

caustic
[kɔ́:stik]

a. 신랄한, 빈정대는
A caustic remark is extremely critical, cruel, or bitter.

stitch^{복습}
[stitʃ]

v. 바느질하다, 꿰매다; n. 한 바늘, 한 땀
If you stitch cloth, you use a needle and thread to join two pieces together or to make a decoration.

fling^{복습}
[fliŋ]

vt. (flung-flung) 내던지다, 던지다, (문 등을) 왈칵 열다
If you fling something somewhere, you throw it there using a lot of force.

lunge
[lʌndʒ]

v. 돌진하다, 달려들다; n. 돌입, 돌진
If you lunge in a particular direction, you move in that direction suddenly and clumsily.

subside[*]
[səbsáid]

vi. 가라앉다, 진정되다; 주저앉다; 함몰하다
If a feeling or noise subsides, it becomes less strong or loud.

bend^{※←}
[bend]

n. 커브, 굽음, 굽은 곳; v. 구부리다, 굽히다, 숙이다
A bend in a road, pipe, or other long thin object is a curve or angle in it.

harbor^{※←}
[há:rbər]

n. 항구, 항만
A harbor is an area of the sea at the coast which is partly enclosed by land or strong walls, so that boats can be left there safely.

strident
[stráidənt]

a. 귀에 거슬리는, 소리가 불쾌한
If a voice or sound is strident, it is loud, harsh, and unpleasant to listen to.

din[*]
[din]

n. 소음, 떠듦
A din is a very loud and unpleasant noise that lasts for some time.

kneel^{※←}
[ni:l]

vi. (knelt-knelt) 무릎 꿇다
When you kneel, you bend your legs so that your knees are touching the ground.

quaver[*]
[kwéivər]

vi. (목소리가) 떨리다, 떠는 소리로 말하다; n. 떨리는 소리
If someone's voice quavers, it sounds unsteady, usually because they are nervous or uncertain.

dare^{※←}
[dɛər]

v. 감히 …하다, 무릅쓰다, 도전하다
If you do not dare to do something, you do not have enough courage to do it, or you do not want to do it because you fear the consequences.

relief^{***}
[rilí:f]

n. 안심, 안도
If you feel a sense of relief, you feel happy because something unpleasant has not happened or is no longer happening.

evident^{**}
[évidənt]

a. 분명한, 명백한, 뚜렷한
If something is evident, you notice it easily and clearly.

passageway[*]
[pǽsidʒwèi]

n. 복도; 통로
A passageway is a long narrow space with walls or fences on both sides, which connects one place or room with another.

cabin^{※←}
[kǽbin]

n. 선실, 객실; (통나무) 오두막집
A cabin is a small room in a ship or boat.

puzzle^{※←}
[pʌ́zl]

v. 어리둥절하게 만들다, 곤혹스럽게 하다, 난처하게 하다
(puzzled a. 당혹스러운, 어리둥절한)
If something puzzles you, you do not understand it and feel confused.

grin^{※←}
[grin]

v. (이를 드러내고) 싱긋 웃다, 활짝 웃다; n. 싱긋 웃음
When you grin, you smile broadly.

16.
I Will Tell You Just a Little

1. What did Annemarie do when she got back from Henrik's boat?

    (A) She went to the hospital with Kirsti and Mama.

    (B) She went to sleep.

    (C) She milked the cow.

    (D) She made Kirsti's doll a dress.

2. Where did Henrik hide the Rosens and the other people on his boat?

    (A) Inside a closet

    (B) Underneath the boards of the boat

    (C) Behind some dead fish

    (D) In the boards of the rooftop

3. Who helped Jewish people get onto the fishermen's boats?

    (A) Peter and others in the Resistance

    (B) The fishermen and their families

    (C) The families who lived near the ocean

    (D) Undercover Swedish soldiers

4. Why did the German soldiers use trained dogs?

   (A) The dogs smelled hidden meat and butter on the fishermen's boats.

   (B) The dogs attacked people in the Resistance.

   (C) The dogs attacked fishermen who lied to the German soldiers.

   (D) The dogs could find where people hid on the boats.

5. How did the handkerchief help the Rosens?

   (A) It made the dogs friendly.

   (B) It ruined the dog's sense of smell.

   (C) It made the dogs want to attack the German soldiers.

   (D) The dogs ate the handkerchief instead of finding the people.

6. When did the German soldiers search Henrik's boat?

   (A) When Henrik arrived in Sweden.

   (B) Before Annemarie arrived at the boat.

   (C) About twenty minutes after Annemarie delivered the packet.

   (D) When Henrik was driving the boat to Sweden.

7. How did Henrik know that the Rosens were safe?

   (A) He found them a shelter in Sweden.

   (B) The Rosens stayed with Henrik's family in Sweden.

   (C) He saw people waiting to take the Rosens to a safe shelter.

   (D) He had friends who would help the Rosens run away from the Nazis in Sweden.

☆ *Check Your Reading Speed*

1분에 몇 단어를 읽는지 리딩 속도를 측정해보세요.

$$\frac{1,632 \text{ words}}{\text{reading time ( ) sec}} \times 60 = (\quad) \text{ WPM}$$

☆ *Build Your Vocabulary*

cast***
[kæst]

n. 깁스, 붕대; v. 던지다, 내던지다; 배역을 정하다
A cast is a cover made of plaster which is used to protect a broken bone by keeping part of the body stiff.

footstool
[fútstùːl]

n. 발판
foot (n. 발) + stool (n. 팔걸이가 없는 의자)

hasty**
[héisti]

a. 급한, 성급한 (hastily ad. 급히, 허둥지둥)
A hasty movement, action, or statement is sudden, and often done in reaction to something that has just happened.

barn^{복습}
[baːrn]

n. 헛간, 광
A barn is a building on a farm in which crops or animal food can be kept.

wary
[wéəri]

a. 조심성 있는, 신중한 (warily ad. 조심히, 신중하게)
If you are wary of something or someone, you are cautious because you do not know much about them and you believe they may be dangerous or cause problems.

bucket^{복습}
[bʌ́kit]

n. 양동이, 버킷
A bucket is a round metal or plastic container with a handle attached to its sides.

irritate^{복습}
[írətèit]

vt. 짜증나게 하다, 화나게 하다 (irritated a. 짜증난)
If something irritates you, it keeps annoying you.

snort*
[snɔːrt]

n. 거센 콧김; v. 콧김을 뿜다, (경멸 등으로) 콧방귀 뀌다
A snort is a rough, noisy sound made by breathing forcefully through the nostrils.

toss^{복습}
[tɔːs]

v. 던지다, 내던지다
If you toss something somewhere, you throw it there lightly, often in a rather careless way.

rhythmic^{복습}
[ríðmik]

a. 주기적인; 율동적인
A rhythmic movement or sound is repeated at regular intervals, forming a regular pattern or beat.

announce^{복습}
[ənáuns]

vt. 알리다, 공고하다, 전하다
If you announce a piece of news or an intention, especially something that people may not like, you say it loudly and clearly, so that everyone you are with can hear it.

squirt
[skwə:rt]

v. 분출하다, 뿜어 나오다
If you squirt a liquid somewhere or if it squirts somewhere, the liquid comes out of a narrow opening in a thin fast stream.

grumble**
[grʌ́mbəl]

v. 투덜거리다, 불평하다; n. 투덜댐, 불평
If someone grumbles, they complain about something in a bad-tempered way.

spoon
[spu:n]

vt. 숟가락으로 뜨다; n. 숟가락, 스푼
If you spoon food into something, you put it there with a spoon.

prop
[prɑp]

v. 받치다, 기대 세우다, 버티다; n. 지주, 버팀목
If you prop an object on or against something, you support it by putting something underneath it or by resting it somewhere.

nurse
[nə:rs]

n. 간호사; vt. 간호하다; 젖 먹이다
A nurse is a person whose job is to care for people who are ill.

hesitate
[hézətèit]

v. 주저하다, 머뭇거리다, 망설이다
If you hesitate, you do not speak or act for a short time, usually because you are uncertain, embarrassed, or worried about what you are going to say or do.

argue
[ɑ́:rgju:]

v. 논쟁하다, 주장하다
If one person argues with another, they speak angrily to each other about something that they disagree about.

misty
[místi]

a. 안개가 짙은, 안개 자욱한
On a misty day, there is a lot of mist in the air.

stack
[stæk]

v. 쌓다, 쌓아올리다; n. 더미; 많음, 다량
If you stack a number of things, you arrange them in neat piles.

hay
[hei]

n. 건초, 건초용 풀
Hay is grass which has been cut and dried so that it can be used to feed animals.

frighten
[fráitn]

v. 놀라게 하다, 섬뜩하게 하다; 기겁하다 (frightened a. 깜짝 놀란, 겁이 난)
If something or someone frightens you, they cause you to suddenly feel afraid, anxious, or nervous.

interrupt
[ìntərʌ́pt]

v. 방해하다, 가로막다, 저지하다
If you interrupt someone who is speaking, you say or do something that causes them to stop.

startle
[stɑ́:rtl]

v. 깜짝 놀라게 하다; 움찔하다; n. 깜짝 놀람 (startled a. 놀란)
If something sudden and unexpected startles you, it surprises and frightens you slightly.

figure out

phrasal v. …을 생각해내다, 발견하다
If you figure out a solution to a problem or the reason for something, you succeed in solving it or understanding it.

frown
[fraun]

vi. 얼굴을 찡그리다, 눈살을 찌푸리다; n. 찌푸린 얼굴
When someone frowns, their eyebrows become drawn together, because they are annoyed or puzzled.

drug[**]
[drʌg]
v. 약을 먹이다; n. 약; 마약
If you drug a person or animal, you give them a chemical substance in order to make them sleepy or unconscious.

widen[적중]
[wáidn]
v. 넓히다, 넓게 되다
If your eyes widen, they open more.

rare[**]
[rɛər]
a. 드문, 진귀한 (rarely ad. 드물게, 진귀하게)
An event or situation that is rare does not occur very often.

conceal[**]
[kənsíːl]
vt. 감추다, 비밀로 하다
If you conceal something, you cover it or hide it carefully.

pile[적중]
[pail]
v. 쌓아 올리다; 쌓이다; n. 쌓아 올린 더미, 다수
If you pile things somewhere, you put them there so that they form a mass of them that is high in the middle and has sloping sides.

deck[***]
[dek]
n. 갑판
A deck on a vehicle such as a bus or ship is a lower or upper area of it.

confront[**]
[kənfrʌnt]
vt. 마주하다, 직면하다
If you confront someone, you stand or sit in front of them, especially when you are going to fight, argue, or compete with them.

handker-chief[적중]
[hǽŋkərtʃif]
n. 손수건
A handkerchief is a small square piece of fabric which you use for blowing your nose.

pail[적중]
[peil]
n. 들통, 버킷
A pail is a bucket, usually made of metal or wood.

udder[적중]
[ʌ́dər]
n. (소·양·염소 등의) 젖통
A cow's udder is the organ that hangs below its body and produces milk.

damp[적중]
[dæmp]
a. 축축한; n. 습기
Something that is damp is slightly wet.

scent[적중]
[sent]
n. 냄새, 향기; v. 냄새 맡다; 냄새를 풍기다
The scent of a person or animal is the smell that they leave and that other people sometimes follow when looking for them.

attract[**]
[ətrǽkt]
vt. 끌다, 끌어당기다; 마음을 끌다
If something attracts people or animals, it has features that cause them to come to it.

ruin[적중]
[rúːin]
v. 망치다, 못쓰게 만들다; 몰락하다; n. 파멸, 멸망
To ruin something means to severely harm, damage, or spoil it.

lunge[적중]
[lʌndʒ]
v. 돌진하다, 달려들다; n. 돌입, 돌진
If you lunge in a particular direction, you move in that direction suddenly and clumsily.

roam[**]
[roum]
vi. 거닐다, 배회하다
If you roam an area or roam around it, you wander or travel around it without having a particular purpose.

dock^{복습}
[dɑk]

n. 선창, 부두; v. 부두에 들어가다; (우주선이) 도킹하다
A dock is an enclosed area in a harbor where ships go to be loaded, unloaded, and repaired.

halt^{복습}
[hɔːlt]

v. 멈추다, 정지하다; n. 정지, 휴식, 멈춤
When a person or a vehicle halts or when something halts them, they stop moving in the direction they were going and stand still.

trail off

phrasal v. (목소리가) 서서히 사라지다 (trail v. 끌다; 뒤쫓다)
If a speaker's voice or a speaker trails off, their voice becomes quieter and they hesitate until they stop speaking completely.

whirl**
[hwəːrl]

v. 빙글 돌다, 선회하다
If something or someone whirls around or if you whirl them around, they move around or turn around very quickly.

pat^{복습}
[pæt]

v. 톡톡 가볍게 치다, (애정을 담아) 쓰다듬다; n. 쓰다듬기
If you pat something or someone, you tap them lightly, usually with your hand held flat.

ashore**
[əʃɔ́ːr]

ad. 해안으로, 물가에
Someone or something that comes ashore comes from the sea onto the shore.

shelter***
[ʃéltər]

n. 피난처, 은신처
A small place which is made to protect people from bad weather or danger.

invade**
[invéid]

v. 침입하다, 침략하다
To invade a country means to enter it by force with an army.

complicated**
[kɑ́mpləkèitid]

a. 복잡한, 이해하기 어려운
If you say that something is complicated, you mean it has so many parts or aspects that it is difficult to understand or deal with.

murmur^{복습}
[mə́ːrmər]

v. 중얼거리다; 투덜거리다; n. 중얼거림
If you murmur something, you say it very quietly, so that not many people can hear what you are saying.

cramped
[kræmpt]

a. 비좁은, 답답한, 꽉 끼는
A cramped room or building is not big enough for the people or things in it.

seasick*
[síːsìk]

a. 뱃멀미가 난, 뱃멀미의
If someone is seasick when they are travelling in a boat, they vomit or feel sick because of the way the boat is moving.

courageous^{복습}
[kəréidʒəs]

a. 용기 있는, 용감한, 담력이 있는
Someone who is courageous shows courage.

stretch^{복습}
[stretʃ]

v. 잡아 늘이다, 쭉 펴다; n. 뻗침
When you stretch, you put your arms or legs out straight and tighten your muscles.

shriek^{복습}
[ʃriːk]

v. 새된 소리를 지르다, 비명을 지르다; n. 비명
When someone shrieks, they make a short, very loud cry.

17.
All This Long Time

1. What did Mama do for the Rosens while they were away?

    (A) She made them new clothing.
    (B) She kept the furniture and candlesticks inside their apartment
       clean.
    (C) She planned a party for the day they could return to
       Copenhagen.
    (D) She wrote them letters every week telling them about
       Copenhagen.

2. How did Peter Neilsen die?

    (A) He was captured and then executed by the Germans in a public
       square.
    (B) He was caught in a secret hiding place and shot by the Germans.
    (C) He was captured when helping Jewish people go to Henrik's
       boat.
    (D) He was shot and killed while running away from the Germans
       in Copenhagen.

3. Peter Neilsen was buried _____.

   (A) near Henrik's house
   (B) beside Lise
   (C) where he was killed
   (D) in a cemetery near Annemarie's apartment

4. Annemarie learned that Lise was _____.

   (A) not actually hit by a car
   (B) Peter were not really engaged
   (C) part of the Resistance
   (D) shot in the arm by the Germans

5. How was Lise killed?

   (A) She was shot by the Germans in an alleyway.
   (B) She was executed in a public square.
   (C) She was killed in a cellar where she attended secret meetings.
   (D) She was hit and killed by a German military car.

6. Ellen's necklace was hidden _____.

   (A) inside the pocket of Lise's dress
   (B) behind Annemarie's dolls
   (C) inside Annemarie's pillow
   (D) inside a chest at Henrik's house

7. What will Annemarie do with Ellen's necklace?

   (A) She will wear it until Ellen returns home.
   (B) She will mail it to Ellen.
   (C) She will leave it inside Ellen's apartment.
   (D) She will give it to her father.

1분에 몇 단어를 읽는지 리딩 속도를 측정해보세요.

$$\frac{900 \text{ words}}{\text{reading time ( ) sec}} \times 60 = (\quad) \text{ WPM}$$

✿ *Build Your Vocabulary*

weep^{복습}
[wiːp]

v. (wept-wept) 눈물을 흘리다, 울다
If someone weeps, they cry.

anthem**
[ǽnθəm]

n. 성가, 찬송가 (national anthem n. 국가)
An anthem is a song which is used to represent a particular nation, society, or group and which is sung on special occasions.

balcony^{복습}
[bǽlkəni]

n. 발코니; (극장의) 2층 특별석
A balcony is a platform on the outside of a building, above ground level, with a wall or railing around it.

banner**
[bǽnər]

n. 기(旗); 현수막
A banner is a long strip of cloth with something written on it.

tend**
[tend]

① vt. (기계·식물 등을) 손질하다, 돌보다, 기르다 ② vi. 향하다, 경향이 있다
If you tend someone or something, you do what is necessary to keep them in a good condition or to improve their condition.

polish^{복습}
[pális]

v. 닦다, 윤내다; n. 광택; 세련
If you polish something, you rub it with a cloth to make it shine.

flee^{복습}
[fliː]

vi. (fled-fled) 달아나다, 도망하다, 내빼다
If you flee from something or someone, or flee a person or thing, you escape from them.

unoccupied*
[ʌnákjəpàid]

a. 소유자가 없는
If a building is unoccupied, there is nobody in it.

lighthearted^{복습}
[láithá:rtid]

a. 근심 걱정 없는, 마음 편한; 쾌활한, 명랑한
Someone who is lighthearted is cheerful and happy.

chatterbox^{복습}
[tʃǽtərbàks]

n. 수다쟁이
A chatterbox is someone who talks a lot.

recall***
[rikɔ́ːl]

vt. 생각해내다, 상기하다, 소환하다; n. 회상, 상기
When you recall something, you remember it and tell others about it.

force^{복습}
[fɔːrs]

vt. 억지로 …시키다, 강요하다; n. 힘, 폭력, 군사력
If someone forces you to do something, they make you do it even though you do not want to.

devastate*
[dévəstèit]

vt. 완전히 파괴하다; 엄청난 충격을 주다, 비탄에 빠뜨리다
(devastating a. 통렬한, 충격적인)
You can use devastating to emphasize that something is very shocking, upsetting, or terrible.

capture**
[kǽptʃər]

vt. 붙잡다, 사로잡다; 포착하다; n. 포획; 포착
If you capture someone or something, you catch them, especially in a war.

execute**
[éksikjù:t]

vt. 처형하다; 실행하다, 집행하다
To execute someone means to kill them as a punishment for a serious crime.

square***
[skwɛər]

n. 광장; 정사각형; a. 정사각형의; 공명정대한
In a town or city, a square is a flat open place, often in the shape of a square.

for the sake of

idiom ···을 위하여
If you do something for the sake of something, you do it for that purpose or in order to achieve that result.

bury***
[béri]

vt. 묻다, 파묻다, 매장하다
To bury a dead person means to put their body into a grave and cover it with earth.

grave***
[greiv]

① n. 무덤, 묘 ② a. 중대한, 근엄한
A grave is a place where a dead person is buried.

bleak*
[bli:k]

a. 황량한, 처량한, 삭막한
If you describe a place as bleak, you mean that it looks cold, empty, and unattractive.

bear***
[bɛər]

① v. 견디다; (의무 · 책임을) 지다; 지니다; 낳다 ② n. 곰
If you bear an unpleasant experience, you accept it because you are unable to do anything about it.

cellar**
[sélər]

n. 지하 저장실
A cellar is a room underneath a building, which is often used for storing things in.

raid*
[reid]

vt. 급습하다, 침입하다; n. 급습, 습격
If the police raid a building, they enter it suddenly and by force in order to look for dangerous criminals or for evidence of something illegal, such as drugs or weapons.

bandage**
[bǽndidʒ]

vt. ···에 붕대를 감다; n. 붕대; 안대
If you bandage a wound or part of someone's body, you tie a bandage around it.

sling*
[sliŋ]

n. 어깨에 메는 붕대; 투석기; vt. 던져 올리다, 투석기로 쏘다
A sling is a piece of cloth which supports someone's broken or injured arm and is tied round their neck.

funeral^{복습}
[fjú:nərəl]

n. 장례식
A ceremony for burying or burning the body of a dead person.

blur [blə:r]
n. 흐림, 침침함; 더러움, 얼룩; v. (광경 · 의식 · 눈 등을) 흐리게 하다
A blur is a shape or area which you cannot see clearly because it has no distinct outline or because it is moving very fast.

grief [gri:f]
n. 슬픔, 비탄
Grief is a feeling of extreme sadness.

blink [bliŋk]
v. 눈을 깜박거리다; (등불 · 별 등이) 깜박이다; n. 깜박거림
When you blink or when you blink your eyes, you shut your eyes and very quickly open them again.

amid [əmíd]
prep. … 의 한복판에; …이 한창일 때에
If something happens amid noises or events of some kind, it happens while the other things are happening.

announce [ənáuns]
vt. 알리다, 공고하다, 전하다
If you announce a piece of news or an intention, especially something that people may not like, you say it loudly and clearly, so that everyone you are with can hear it.

engagement [engéidʒmənt]
n. 약혼; 약속, 계약
An engagement is an agreement that two people have made with each other to get married.

trunk [trʌŋk]
n. 여행 가방; (나무의) 줄기, 몸뚱이
A trunk is a large, strong case or box used for storing things or for taking on a journey.

fade [feid]
vi. 바래다, 시들다, 희미해지다
When a colored object fades or when the light fades it, it gradually becomes paler.

discolor [diskʌ́lər]
v. 변색시키다; 빛깔이 바래다
If something discolors or if it is discolored by something else, its original color changes, so that it looks unattractive.

lain [lein]
LIE (vi. 눕다; 위치하다)의 과거분사
If an object lies in a particular place, it is in a flat position in that place.

necklace [néklis]
n. 목걸이
A necklace is a piece of jewelry such as a chain or a string of beads which someone, usually a woman, wears round their neck.

gleam [gli:m]
vi. 빛나다, 반짝이다, 번득이다; n. 번득임, 어스레한 빛
If an object or a surface gleams, it reflects light because it is shiny and clean.

rejoice [ridʒɔ́is]
v. 기뻐하다; 즐겁게 하다
If you rejoice, you are very pleased about something and you show it in your behavior.

crowd [kraud]
n. 군중, 인파; v. 군집하다, 붐비다
A crowd is a large group of people who have gathered together, for example to watch or listen to something interesting, or to protest about something.

clasp ^{중급}
[klæsp]

n. 걸쇠, 버클; 악수, 포옹; v. 고정시키다, 죄다; 꼭 쥐다, 악수하다
A clasp is a small device that fastens something.

1분에 몇 단어를 읽는지 리딩 속도를 측정해보세요.

$$\frac{1{,}032 \text{ words}}{\text{reading time ( ) sec}} \times 60 = (\qquad) \text{ WPM}$$

✿ *Build Your Vocabulary*

dedicate**
[dédikèit]

vt. 헌납하다, (시간 · 생애 등을) 바치다
If someone dedicates something such as a book, play, or piece of music to you, they mention your name, for example in the front of a book or when a piece of music is performed, as a way of showing affection or respect for you.

occupation^{복습}
[àkjəpéiʃən]

n. 점령, 점거; 직업, 업무
The occupation of a country happens when it is entered and controlled by a foreign army.

fascinate^{복습}
[fǽsənèit]

v. 매혹하다, 반하게 하다; 주의를 끌다 (fascinated a. 매혹된, 마음을 빼앗긴)
If something fascinates you, it interests and delights you so much that your thoughts tend to concentrate on it.

description^{복습}
[diskrípʃən]

n. 서술, 기술, 묘사
A description of someone or something is an account which explains what they are or what they look like.

deprivation
[dèprəvéiʃən]

n. 박탈, 탈취; 상실, 손실
If you suffer deprivation, you do not have or are prevented from having something that you want or need.

sacrifice***
[sǽkrəfàis]

n. 희생; v. 희생하다, 제물로 바치다
Sacrifice is the act of giving up something that is valuable or important, usually to obtain something else for yourself or for other people.

integrity*
[intégrəti]

n. 진실성, 온전함, 고결, 성실
The integrity of something such as a group of people or a text is its state of being a united whole.

surrender^{복습}
[səréndər]

v. 항복하다, 내어주다, 넘겨주다; n. 항복, 굴복
If you surrender, you stop fighting or resisting someone and agree that you have been beaten.

undefended
[ʌndiféndid]

a. 방비가 없는, 보호받지 않고 있는
If something is undefended, it is not protected or guarded.

sorrow***
[sárou]

n. 슬픔, 비애, 비통
Sorrow is a feeling of deep sadness or regret.

arm***
[ɑːrm]

① vt. 무장시키다; n. 무기 ② n. 팔
If you arm someone with a weapon, you provide them with a weapon.

spit-shine
[spítʃàin]

v. (구두 등을 침을 발라 닦아서) 번쩍번쩍하게 하다
spit (n. 침) + shine (v. 빛나다)

charming**
[tʃáːrmiŋ]

a. 매력 있는, 매력적인
If you say that something is charming, you mean that it is very pleasant or attractive.

a flight of fancy

idiom 상상의 나래
A flight of fancy is an idea or a statement that is very imaginative but not practical or sensible.

navy복습
[néivi]

n. 해군; 짙은 남색
A country's navy consists of the people it employs to fight at sea, and the ships they use.

harbor복습
[háːrbər]

n. 항구, 항만
A harbor is an area of the sea at the coast which is partly enclosed by land or strong walls, so that boats can be left there safely.

explosion복습
[iksplóuʒən]

n. 폭발
An explosion is a sudden, violent burst of energy, for example one caused by a bomb.

fierce복습
[fiərs]

a. 격렬한, 지독한; 사나운 (fiercely ad. 맹렬하게)
Fierce conditions are very intense, great, or strong.

worship***
[wə́ːrʃip]

v. 예배하다, 숭배하다
If you worship a god, you show your respect to the god, for example by saying prayers.

fictional*
[fíkʃənəl]

a. 꾸며낸, 허구의; 소설적인
Fictional characters or events occur only in stories, plays, or films and never actually existed or happened.

relocate복습
[riːlóukeit]

v. (주거·공장·주민 등을) 다시 배치하다, 이전시키다
If people or businesses relocate or if someone relocates them, they move to a different place.

compassion*
[kəmpǽʃən]

n. 동정심, 연민
Compassion is a feeling of pity, sympathy, and understanding for someone who is suffering.

flee복습
[fliː]

vi. (fled-fled) 달아나다, 도망하다, 내빼다
If you flee from something or someone, or flee a person or thing, you escape from them.

raid복습
[reid]

n. 급습, 습격, 침입; vt. 급습하다, 침입하다
A raid is a sudden armed attack with the aim of causing damage rather than occupying any of the enemy's land.

population***
[pàpjəléiʃən]

n. 인구; 주민
The population of a country or area is all the people who live in it.

smuggle*
[smʌ́gəl]

v. 밀입국하다, 밀항하다; 밀수하다
If someone smuggles things or people into a place or out of it, they take them there illegally or secretly.

hem^{빈출}
[hem]

vt. 옷단을 대다; 둘러싸다; n. (천 · 옷의) 옷단, 가장자리

If you hem something, you form a hem along its edge.

heroine**
[hérouin]

n. 여주인공, 영웅적인 여자

The heroine of a book, play, film, or story is the main female character, who usually has good qualities.

sniff^{빈출}
[snif]

v. 냄새를 맡다, 코를 킁킁거리다; 콧방귀를 뀌다; n. 냄새 맡음; 콧방귀

If you sniff something or sniff at it, you smell it by breathing air through your nose.

swift^{빈출}
[swift]

a. 빠른, 신속한 (swiftly ad. 빨리, 즉시)

A swift event or process happens very quickly or without delay.

detection
[ditékʃən]

n. 탐지, 간파, 발각

Detection is the act of noticing or sensing something.

compose**
[kəmpóuz]

vt. 구성하다, 조립하다, 만들다

The things that something is composed of are its parts or members.

attract^{빈출}
[ətrǽkt]

vt. 끌다, 끌어당기다; 마음을 끌다

If something attracts people or animals, it has features that cause them to come to it.

numb*
[nʌm]

vt. 감각을 잃게 하다; 망연자실케 하다; a. 감각을 잃은

If cold weather, a drug, or a blow numbs a part of your body, you can no longer feel anything in it.

temporary***
[témpərèri]

a. 일시의, 임시의, 한때의 (temporarily ad. 일시적으로)

Something that is temporary lasts for only a limited time.

permeate*
[pə́:rmièit]

v. 스며들다, 침투하다, 퍼지다

If something permeates a place, it spreads throughout it.

device**
[diváis]

n. 장치, 설비

A device is an object that has been invented for a particular purpose.

operation***
[àpəréiʃən]

n. 작전; 작용, 작동; 시행

An operation is a highly organized activity that involves many people doing different things.

orchestrate
[ɔ́:rkəstrèit]

v. 조직하다, 획책하다; 관현악용으로 편곡하다

If you say that someone orchestrates an event or situation, you mean that they carefully organize it in a way that will produce the result that they want.

represent***
[rèprizént]

vt. 나타내다, 표현하다; 대표하다

To represent an idea or quality means to be a symbol or an expression of that idea or quality.

courageous^{빈출}
[kəréidʒəs]

a. 용기 있는, 용감한, 담력이 있는

Someone who is courageous shows courage.

idealistic
[aidìːəlístik]

a. 이상주의적인, 이상주의의
If you describe someone as idealistic, you mean that they have ideals, and base their behavior on these ideals, even though this may be impractical.

eventually**
[ivéntʃuəli]

ad. 결국, 마침내
Eventually means at the end of a situation or process or as the final result of it.

capture****
[kǽptʃər]

vt. 붙잡다, 사로잡다; 포착하다; n. 포획; 포착
If you capture someone or something, you catch them, especially in a war.

execute****
[éksikjùːt]

vt. 처형하다; 실행하다, 집행하다
To execute someone means to kill them as a punishment for a serious crime.

skim**
[skim]

vt. 훑어보다; 스쳐지나가다, 미끄러지듯 가다
If you skim a piece of writing, you read through it quickly.

sabotage****
[sǽbətɑ̀ːʒ]

n. 방해 행위, 파괴 행위, 사보타주
A sabotage is an act to deliberately damage or destroy something in order to hurt.

tactic*
[tǽktik]

n. 전술
Tactics are the methods that you choose to use in order to achieve what you want in a particular situation.

routine**
[ruːtíːn]

n. 판에 박힌 일
A routine is the usual series of things that you do at a particular time.

unwavering****
[ʌnwéivəriŋ]

a. 동요하지 않는, 확고한, 의연한
If you describe a feeling or attitude as unwavering, you mean that it is strong and firm and does not weaken.

determination**
[ditə̀ːrmənéiʃən]

n. 결심, 결단, 결정
Determination is the quality that you show when you have decided to do something and you will not let anything stop you.

boyish
[bɔ́iiʃ]

a. 소년 같은, 소년다운
If you describe a man as boyish, you mean that he is like a boy in his appearance or behavior, and you find this characteristic quite attractive.

determined****
[ditə́ːrmind]

a. 결연한, 굳게 결심한
If you are determined to do something, you have made a firm decision to do it and will not let anything stop you.

decency*
[díːsnsi]

n. 품위, 체면; 예의, 예절
Decency is the quality of following accepted moral standards.

narrow-minded*
[nǽroumáindid]

a. 마음이 좁은, 옹졸한, 편협한
If you describe someone as narrow-minded, you are criticizing them because they are unwilling to consider new ideas or other people's opinions.

prejudice^{**}
[prédʒədis]

vt. 편견을 갖게 하다; n. 편견, 선입견
A person who is prejudiced against someone has an unreasonable dislike of them.

hunger^{**}
[hʌ́ŋgər]

v. 갈망하다; 굶주리다; n. 굶주림; 갈망, 열망
If you say that someone hungers for something, you are emphasizing that they want it very much.

peasant^{**}
[pézənt]

n. 소작농, 농부
A peasant is a poor person of low social status who works on the land; used of people who live in countries where farming is still a common way of life.

look forward to^{복습}

idiom ···을 기대하다, 고대하다
If you say that someone is looking forward to something useful or positive, you mean they expect it to happen.

remind^{복습}
[rimáind]

vt. 생각나게 하다, 상기시키다, 일깨우다
If someone reminds you of a fact or event that you already know about, they say something which makes you think about it.

수고하셨습니다!

드디어 끝까지 다 읽으셨군요! 축하드립니다! 여러분은 이 책을 통해 총 27,197개의 단어를 읽으셨고, 830개 이상의 어휘와 표현들을 익히셨습니다. 이 책에 나온 어휘는 다른 원서를 읽을 때에도 빈번히 만날 수 있는 필수 어휘들입니다. 이 책을 읽었던 경험은 비슷한 수준의 다른 원서들을 읽을 때 큰 도움이 될 것입니다.

이제 자신의 상황에 맞게 원서를 반복해서 읽거나, 오디오북을 들어 볼 수 있습니다. 혹은 비슷한 수준의 다른 원서를 찾아 읽는 것도 좋습니다. 일단 원서를 완독한 뒤에 어떻게 계속 영어 공부를 이어갈 수 있을지, 도움말을 꼼꼼히 살펴보고 각자 상황에 맞게 적용해 보세요!

리딩(Reading)을 확실하게 다지고 싶다면? 반복해서 읽어 보세요!

리딩 실력을 탄탄하게 다지고 싶다면, 같은 원서를 2~3번 반복해서 읽을 것을 권합니다. 같은 책을 여러 번 읽으면 지루할 것 같지만, 꼭 그렇지도 않습니다. 반복해서 읽을 때 처음과 주안점을 다르게 두면, 전혀 다른 느낌으로 재미있게 읽을 수 있습니다.

처음 원서를 읽을 때는 생소한 단어들과 스토리로 인해 읽으면서 곧바로 이해하기가 매우 힘들 수 있습니다. 전체 맥락을 잡고 읽어도 약간 버거운 느낌이지요. 하지만 반복해서 읽기 시작하면 달라집니다. 일단 내용을 파악한 상황이기 때문에 문장 구조나 어휘의 활용에 더 집중하게 되고, 조금 더 깊이 있게 읽을 수 있습니다. 좋은 표현과 문장을 수집하고 메모할 만한 여유도 생기게 되지요. 어휘도 많이 익숙해졌기 때문에 리딩 속도에도 탄력이 붙습니다. 처음 읽을 때는 '내용'에서 재미를 느꼈다면, 반복해서 읽을 때에는 '영어'에서 재미를 느끼게 되는 것입니다. 따라서 리딩 실력을 더욱 확고하게 다지고자 한다면, 같은 책을 2~3회 정도 반복해서 읽을 것을 권해 드립니다.

리스닝(Listening) 실력을 늘리고 싶다면?
귀를 통해서 읽어 보세요!

많은 영어 학습자들이 '리스닝이 안 돼서 문제'라고 한탄합니다. 그리고 리스닝 실력을 늘리는 방법으로 무슨 뜻인지 몰라도 반복해서 듣는 '무작정 듣기'를 선택합니다. 하지만 뜻도 모르면서 무작정 듣는 일에는 엄청난 인내력이 필요합니다. 그래서 대부분 며칠 시도하다가 포기해 버리고 말지요.

따라서 모르는 내용을 무작정 듣는 것보다는 어느 정도 알고 있는 내용을 반복해서 듣는 것이 더 효과적인 듣기 방법입니다. 그리고 이런 방식의 듣기에 활용할 수 있는 가장 좋은 교재가 오디오북입니다.

리스닝 실력을 향상하고 싶다면, 이 책에서 제공하는 오디오북을 이용해서 듣는 연습을 해 보세요. 활용법은 간단합니다. 일단 책을 한 번 완독했다면, 오디오북을 통해 다시 들어 보는 것입니다. 휴대 기기에 넣어 시간이 날 때 틈틈이 듣는 것도 좋고, 책상에 앉아 눈으로는 텍스트를 보며 귀로 읽는 것도 좋습니다. 이미 읽었던 내용이라 이해하기가 훨씬 수월하고, 애매했던 발음들도 자연스럽게 교정할 수 있습니다. 또 성우의 목소리 연기를 듣다 보면 내용이 더욱 생동감 있게 다가와 이해도가 높아지는 효과도 거둘 수 있습니다.

반대로 듣기에 자신 있는 사람이라면, 책을 읽기 전에 처음부터 오디오북을 먼저 듣는 것도 좋은 방법입니다. 귀를 통해 책을 쭉 읽어 보고, 이후에 다시 눈으로 책을 읽으면서 잘 들리지 않았던 부분을 보충하는 것이지요.

중요한 것은 내용을 따라가면서, 내용에 푹 빠져서 반복해 들어야 한다는 것입니다. 이렇게 연습을 반복해서 눈으로 읽지 않은 책이라도 '귀를 통해' 읽을 수 있을 정도가 되면, 리스닝으로 고생하는 일은 거의 없을 것입니다.

왼쪽의 QR 코드를 스마트폰으로 인식하여 정식 오디오북을 들어 보세요! 더불어 롱테일북스 홈페이지(www.longtailbooks.co.kr)에서도 오디오북 MP3 파일을 다운로드 받을 수 있습니다.

스피킹(Speaking)이 고민이라면? 소리 내어 읽어 보세요!

스피킹 역시 많은 학습자들이 고민하는 부분입니다. 스피킹이 고민이라면, 원서를 큰 소리로 읽는 낭독 훈련(Voice Reading)을 해 보세요!

'소리 내어 읽는 것이 말하기에 정말로 도움이 될까?'라고 의아한 생각이 들 수도 있습니다. 하지만 인간의 두뇌 입장에서 봤을 때, 성대 구조를 활용해서 '발화'한다는 점에서는 소리 내어 읽기와 말하기에 큰 차이가 없다고 합니다. 소리 내어 읽는 것은 '타인의 생각'을 전달하고, 직접 말하는 것은 '자신의 생각'을 전달한다는 차이가 있을 뿐, 머릿속에서 문장을 처리하고 조음기관(혀와 성대 등)을 움직여 의미를 만든다는 점에서 같은 과정인 것이지요. 따라서 소리 내어 읽는 연습을 꾸준히 하는 것은 스피킹 연습에 큰 도움이 됩니다.

소리 내어 읽기를 하는 방법은 간단합니다. 일단 오디오북을 들으면서 성우의 목소리를 최대한 따라 하며 같이 읽어 보세요. 발음뿐 아니라 억양, 어조, 느낌까지 완벽히 따라 한다고 생각하면서 소리 내어 읽습니다. 따라 읽는 것이 조금 익숙해지면, 옆의 누군가에게 이 책을 읽어 준다는 생각으로 소리 내어 계속 읽어 나갑니다. 한 번 눈과 귀로 읽었던 책이기 때문에 보다 수월하게 진행할 수 있고, 자연스럽게 어휘와 표현을 복습하는 효과도 거두게 됩니다. 또 이렇게 소리 내어 읽은 것을 녹음해서 들어 보면 스스로에게도 좋은 피드백이 됩니다.

최근 말하기가 강조되면서 소리 내어 읽기가 크게 각광을 받고 있긴 하지만, 그렇다고 소리 내어 읽기가 무조건 좋은 것만은 아닙니다. 책을 소리 내어 읽다 보면, 무의식적으로 속으로 발음을 하는 습관을 가지게 되어 리딩 속도 자체는 오히려 크게 떨어지는 현상이 발생할 수 있습니다. 따라서 빠른 리딩 속도가 중요한 수험생이나 고학력 학습자들에게는 소리 내어 읽기가 적절하지 않은 방법입니다. 효과가 좋다는 말만 믿고 무턱대고 따라 하기보다는 자신의 필요에 맞게 우선순위를 정하고 원서를 활용하는 것이 좋습니다.

※이 책 Number The Stars는 소리 내어 읽기에 적절하지 않은 책입니다. 소리 내어 읽기를 한다면, 더 짧고 간단한 책을 골라 보세요!

라이팅(Writing)까지 욕심이 난다면? 요약하는 연습을 해 보세요!

원서를 라이팅 연습에 직접적으로 활용하는 데에는 한계가 있지만, 적절히 활용하면 원서도 유용한 라이팅 자료가 될 수 있습니다.

특히 책을 읽고 그 내용을 요약하는 연습은 큰 도움이 됩니다. 요약 훈련의 방식도 간단합니다. 원서를 읽고 그날 읽은 분량만큼 혹은 책을 다 읽고 전체 내용을 기반으로, 책 내용을 한번 요약하고 나의 느낌을 영어로 적어 보는 것입니다.

이때 그 책에 나왔던 단어와 표현을 최대한 활용하여 요약하는 것이 중요합니다. 영어 표현력은 결국 얼마나 다양한 어휘로 많은 표현을 해 보았느냐가 좌우하게 됩니다. 이런 면에서 내가 읽은 책을, 그 책에 나온 문장과 어휘로 다시 표현해 보는 것은 매우 효율적인 방법입니다. 책에 나온 어휘와 표현을 단순히 읽고 무슨 말인지 아는 정도가 아니라, 실제로 직접 활용해서 쓸 수 있을 만큼 확실하게 익히게 되는 것이지요. 여기에 첨삭까지 받을 수 있는 방법이 있다면 금상첨화입니다.

이러한 '표현하기' 연습은 스피킹 훈련에도 그대로 적용될 수 있습니다. 책을 읽고 그 내용을 3분 안에 다른 사람에게 영어로 말하는 연습을 해 보세요. 순발력과 표현력을 기르는 좋은 훈련이 될 것입니다.

꾸준히 원서를 읽고 싶다면? 뉴베리 수상작을 계속 읽어 보세요!

뉴베리 상이 세계 최고 권위의 아동 문학상인 만큼, 그 수상작들은 확실히 완성도를 검증받은 작품이라고 할 수 있습니다. 특히 '쉬운 어휘로 쓰인 깊이 있는 문장'으로 이루어졌다는 점이 영어 학습자들에게 큰 호응을 얻고 있습니다. 이렇게 '검증된 원서'를 꾸준히 읽는 것은 영어 실력 향상에 큰 도움이 됩니다.

아래에 수준별로 제시된 뉴베리 수상작 목록을 보며 적절한 책들을 찾아 계속 읽어 보세요. 꼭 뉴베리 수상작이 아니더라도 마음에 드는 작가의 다른 책을 읽어 보는 것 또한 아주 좋은 방법입니다.

• 영어 초보자도 쉽게 읽을 만한 아주 쉬운 수준. 소리 내어 읽기에도 아주 적합.
Sarah, Plain and Tall*(Medal, 8,331단어), The Hundred Penny Box (Honor, 5,878단어), The Hundred Dresses*(Honor, 7,329단어), My Father's Dragon (Honor, 7,682단어), 26 Fairmount Avenue (Honor, 6,737단어)

- 중 · 고등학생 정도 영어 학습자라면 쉽게 읽을 수 있는 수준. 소리 내어 읽기에도 비교적 적합한 편.

Because of Winn-Dixie★(Honor, 22,123단어), What Jamie Saw (Honor, 17,203단어), Charlotte's Web (Honor, 31,938단어), Dear Mr. Henshaw (Medal, 18,145단어), Missing May (Medal, 17,509단어)

- 대학생 정도 영어 학습자라면 무난한 수준. 소리 내어 읽기에는 적합하지 않음.

Number The Stars★(Medal, 27,197단어), A Single Shard (Medal, 33,726단어), The Tale of Despereaux★(Medal, 32,375단어), Hatchet★(Medal, 42,328단어), Bridge to Terabithia (Medal, 32,888단어), A Fine White Dust (Honor, 19,022단어), Jennifer, Hecate, Macbeth, William McKinley and Me, Elizabeth (Honor, 23,266단어)

- 원서 완독 경험을 가진 학습자에게 적절한 수준. 소리 내어 읽기에는 적합하지 않음.

The Giver★(Medal, 43,617단어), From the Mixed-Up Files of Mrs. Basil E. Frankweiler (Medal, 30,906단어), The View from Saturday (Medal, 42,685단어), Holes★(Medal, 47,079단어), Criss Cross (Medal, 48,221단어), Walk Two Moons (Medal, 59,400단어), The Graveyard Book (Medal, 67,380단어)

뉴베리 수상작과 뉴베리 수상 작가의 좋은 작품을 엄선한 「뉴베리 컬렉션」에도 위 목록에 있는 도서 중 상당수가 포함될 예정입니다.

★「뉴베리 컬렉션」으로 이미 출간된 도서

어떤 책들이 출간되었는지 확인하려면, 지금 인터넷 서점에서 뉴베리 컬렉션 을 검색해 보세요.

뉴베리 수상작을 동영상 강의로 만나 보세요!

영어원서 전문 동영상 강의 사이트 영서당(yseodang.com)에서는 뉴베리 컬렉션 『Holes』, 『Because of Winn-Dixie』, 『The Miraculous Journey of Edward Tulane』, 『Wayside School 시리즈』 등의 동영상 강의를 제공하고 있습니다. 뉴베리 수상작이라는 최고의 영어 교재와 EBS 출신 인기 강사가 만난 명강의! 지금 사이트를 방문해서 무료 샘플 강의를 들어 보세요!

'스피드 리딩 카페'를 통해 원서 읽기 습관을 길러 보세요!

일상에서 영어를 한마디도 쓰지 않는 비영어권 국가에서 살고 있는 우리가 영어 환경에 가장 쉽고, 편하고, 부담 없이 노출되는 방법은 바로 '영어원서 읽기'입니다. 언제 어디서든 원서를 붙잡고 읽기만 하면 곧바로 영어를 접하는 환경이 만들어지기 때문이지요. 하루에 20분씩만 꾸준히 읽는다면, 1년에 무려 120시간 동안 영어에 노출될 수 있습니다. 이러한 이유 때문에 영어 교육 전문가들이 영어 원서 읽기를 추천하는 것이지요.
하지만 원서 읽기가 좋다는 것을 알아도 막상 꾸준히 읽는 것은 쉽지 않습니다. 그럴 때에는 13만 명 이상의 회원을 보유한 국내 최대 원서 읽기 동호회 〈스피드 리딩 카페〉(cafe.naver.com/readingtc)를 방문해보세요.
원서별로 정리된 무료 PDF 단어장과 수준별 추천 원서 목록 등 유용한 자료는 물론, 뉴베리 수상작을 포함한 다양한 원서의 리뷰를 무료로 확인할 수 있습니다. 특히 함께 모여서 원서를 읽는 '북클럽'은 중간에 포기하지 않고 원서를 끝까지 읽는 습관을 기르는 데 큰 도움이 될 것입니다.

Answer Key

1. Why Are You Running?

1. A   "We have to practice for the athletic meet on Friday—I know I'm going to win the girls' race this week. I was second last week, but I've been practicing every day. Come on, Ellen," Annemarie pleaded, eyeing the distance to the next corner of the Copenhagen street. "Please?"

2. D   And it meant two rifles, gripped in the hands of the soldiers. She stared at the rifles first. Then, finally, she looked into the face of the soldier who had ordered her to halt.

3. B   His Danish was very poor. Three years, Annemarie thought with contempt. Three years they've been in our country, and still they can't speak our language.

4. A   "Are you going to tell your mother?" Ellen asked Annemarie as they trudged together up the stairs. "I'm not. My mother would be upset."

"No, I won't, either. Mama would probably scold me for running on the street."

...

"Annemarie, what happened? What is Kirsti talking about?" her mother asked anxiously.

5. D   She spoke in a low voice to Ellen's mother. "They must be edgy because of the latest Resistance incidents. Did you read in De Frie Danske about the bombings in Hillerod and Norrebro?"

6. C   But Annemarie heard Mama and Papa talk, sometimes at night, about the news they received that way: news of sabotage against the Nazis, bombs hidden and exploded in the factories that produced war materials, and industrial railroad lines damaged so that the goods couldn't be transported.

7. C   Her mother laughed. "For a little girl, you have a long memory," she told Kirsti. "There hasn't been any butter, or sugar for cupcakes, for a long time. A year, at least."

2. Who Is the Man Who Rides Past?

1. A   All Danish children grew up familiar with fairy tales. Hans Christian Andersen, the most famous of the tale tellers, had been Danish himself.

2. B   She remembered a story that Papa had told her, shortly after the war began, shortly after Denmark had surrendered and the soldiers had moved in overnight to take their places on the corners.

3. A   "He is our king," the boy told the soldier. "He is the King of Denmark."
"Where is his bodyguard?" the soldier had asked. "And do you know what the boy said?" Papa had asked Annemarie. She was sitting on his lap. She was little, then, only seven years old. She shook her head, waiting to hear the answer.
"The boy looked right at the soldier, and he said, 'All of Denmark is his bodyguard.'"

4. B   "Papa," Annemarie had said, finally, into the silence, "sometimes I wonder why the king wasn't able to protect us. Why didn't he fight the Nazis so that they wouldn't come into Denmark with their guns?"
Papa sighed. "We are such a tiny country," he said. "And they are such an enormous enemy. Our king was wise. He knew how few soldiers Denmark had. He knew that many, many Danish people would die if we fought."

5. D   "But not in Sweden!" Annemarie announced, proud that she knew so much about the world. Sweden was blue on the map, and she had seen Sweden, even though she had never been there. Standing behind Uncle Henrik's house, north of Copenhagen, she had looked across the water—the part of the North Sea that was called the Kattegat—to the land on the other side. "That is Sweden you are seeing," Uncle Henrik had told her. "You are looking across to another country."
"That's true," Papa had said. "Sweden is still free."

6. B   It was Lise who was not. It was her tall, beautiful sister who had died in an accident two weeks before her wedding.

7. C   Redheaded Peter, her sister's fiancé, had not married anyone in the years since Lise's death. He had changed a great deal. Once he had been like a fun-loving older brother to Annemarie and Kirsti, teasing and tickling, always a source of foolishness and pranks. Now he still stopped by the apartment often, and his greetings to the girls were warm and smiling, but he was usually in a hurry, talking quickly to Mama and Papa about things Annemarie didn't understand.

3. Where Is Mrs. Hirsch?

1. C The two mothers still had their "coffee" together in the afternoons. They began to knit mittens as the days grew slightly shorter and the first leaves began to fall from the trees, because another winter was coming. Everyone remembered the last one. There was no fuel now for the homes and apartments in Copenhagen, and the winter nights were terribly cold.

2. C But it didn't seem to be the jacket that worried Mama. "Are you sure the sign was in German?" she asked. "Maybe you didn't look carefully."
"Mama, it had a swastika on it."

3. B Peter! She hadn't seen him in a long time. There was something frightening about his being here at night. Copenhagen had a curfew, and no citizens were allowed out after eight o'clock. It was very dangerous, she knew, for Peter to visit at this time.

4. A "Where have you been? We've missed you!"
"My work takes me all over," Peter explained.

5. C "Annemarie," he said, "Peter tells us that the Germans have issued orders closing many stores run by Jews."
"Jews?" Annemarie repeated. "Is Mrs. Hirsch Jewish? Is that why the button shop is closed? Why have they done that?"
Peter leaned forward. "It is their way of tormenting. For some reason, they want to torment Jewish people. It has happened in the other countries. They have taken their time here —have let us relax a little. But now it seems to be starting."

6. B "Papa, do you remember what you heard the boy say to the soldier? That all of Denmark would be the king's bodyguard?"
Her father smiled. "I have never forgotten it," he said.
"Well," Annemarie said slowly, "now I think that all of Denmark must be body-guard for the Jews, as well."

7. D For a moment she felt frightened. But she pulled the blanket up higher around her neck and relaxed. It was all imaginary, anyway—not real. It was only in the fairy tales that people were called upon to be so brave, to die for one another. Not in real-life Denmark. Oh, there were the soldiers; that was true. And the coura-geous Resistance leaders, who sometimes lost their lives; that was true, too.
But ordinary people like the Rosens and the Johansens? Annemarie admitted to herself, snuggling there in the quiet dark, that she was glad to be an ordinary person who would never be called upon for courage.

4. It Will Be a Long Night

1. C   "You know there's no leather anymore," Mama explained. "But they've found a way to make shoes out of fish skin. I don't think these are too ugly."

2. C   Sometimes, Annemarie thought, Kirsti was such a pest, always butting in. But the apartment was small. There was no other place for Kirsti to play. And if they told her to go away, Mama would scold.

3. D   "Silly," Annemarie scoffed. "You never saw the fireworks." Tivoli Gardens was closed now. The German occupation forces had burned part of it, perhaps as a way of punishing the fun-loving Danes for their lighthearted pleasures.

4. D   The next evening's newspaper had told the sad truth. The Danes had destroyed their own naval fleet, blowing up the vessels one by one, as the Germans approached to take over the ships for their own use.

5. A   He turned to her and stroked her hair with his gentle hand. "This morning, at the synagogue, the rabbi told his congregation that the Nazis have taken the synagogue lists of all the Jews. Where they live, what their names are. Of course the Rosens were on that list, along with many others."

6. B   Papa put his arm around her. "They are safe, Ellen. I promise you that. You will see them again quite soon. Can you try hard to believe my promise?"

7. C   "I really don't think anyone will. But it never hurts to be prepared. If anyone should come, even soldiers, you two will be sisters. You are together so much, it will be easy for you to pretend that you are sisters."

5. Who Is the Dark-Haired One?

1. B   "See that blue trunk in the corner?" she said, pointing through the darkness. "Lots of Lise's things are in there. Even her wedding dress.

2. A   "Sophy Rosen is my friend, that is true," Mama said quietly. "Please, could you speak more softly?" My children are asleep."

"Then you will be so kind as to tell me where the Rosens are." He made no effort to lower his voice.

...

Another German voice said, "The Rosens' apartment is empty. We are wondering if they might be visiting their good friends the Johansens."

"Well," said Papa, moving slightly so that he was standing in front of

Annemarie's bedroom door, and she could see nothing except the dark blur of his back, "as you see, you are mistaken. There is no one here but my family."

3. B   Ellen undid her braids, lifted her dark hair away from the thin gold chain she wore around her neck—the chain that held the Star of David—and began to brush her thick curls.

    ...

"Ellen," she whispered urgently, "take your necklace off!"

Ellen's hands flew to her neck. Desperately she began trying to unhook the tiny clasp.

    ...

"Hold still," Annemarie commanded. "This will hurt." She grabbed the little gold chain, yanked with all her strength, and broke it.

4. D   The street soldiers were often young, sometimes ill at ease, and Annemarie remembered how the Giraffe had, for a moment, let his harsh pose slip and had smiled at Kirsti.

But these men were older and their faces were set with anger.

5. B   "You have a blond child sleeping in the other room. And you have this blond daughter—" He gestured toward Annemarie with his head. "Where did you get the dark-haired one?" He twisted the lock of Ellen's hair. "From a different father? From the milkman?"

6. C   "You will see each of my daughters, each with her name written on the photograph," Papa said.

Annemarie knew instantly which photographs he had chosen. The album had many snapshots—all the poorly focused pictures of school events and birthday parties. But it also contained a portrait, taken by a photographer, of each girl as a tiny infant. Mama had written, in her delicate handwriting, the name of each baby daughter across the bottom of those photographs.

7. C   The officer tore the photograph in half and dropped the pieces on the floor.

6. Is the Weather Good for Fishing?

1. A   "Not go to school?" Ellen asked in amazement.

"My parents have always told me that education is the most important thing. Whatever happens, I must get an education."

2. D   Mama put a hand on Papa's arm. "If only I go with the girls, it will be safer. They are unlikely to suspect a woman and her children. But if they are watching us —

if they see all of us leave? If they are aware that the apartment is empty, that you don't go to your office this morning? Then they will know. Then it will be dangerous. I am not afraid to go alone."

3. C   But it wasn't true. Annemarie was quite certain it wasn't true. Cigarettes were the thing that Papa missed, the way Mama missed coffee. He complained often—he had complained only yesterday—that there were no cigarettes in the stores. The men in his office, he said, making a face, smoked almost anything: sometimes dried weeds rolled in paper, and the smell was terrible.

Why was Papa speaking that way, almost as if he were speaking in code?

4. A   Annemarie laughed. "He's my uncle—my mother's brother. And he's a fisherman."

5. D   "And guess what!" Kirsti exclaimed suddenly, in a loud voice, looking at the soldier.

Annemarie's heart sank and she looked at her mother. Mama's eyes were frightened. "Shhh, Kirsti," Mama said. "Don't chatter so."

...

"I'm going to visit my Uncle Henrik," she chirped, "and I'm wearing my brand-new shiny black shoes!"

6. C   The train ride north along the Danish coast was very beautiful.

...

"Come on, girls, we'll walk. It isn't far, just a little under two miles. And it's a nice day. We'll take the path through the woods instead of the road. It's a little longer, but it's so pretty."

7. C   "Didn't you love the castle when we went through Helsingør, Ellen?" Kirsti asked. She had been talking about Kronborg Castle ever since they had seen it, sprawling massive and ancient, beside the sea, from the train.

7. The House by the Sea

1. D   "I have never been this close to the sea," Ellen said.

...

"My mother is afraid of the ocean," she said, laughing. "She says it is too big for her. And too cold!"

2. B   "Maybe. I can't tell. They're too far away. Uncle Henrik's boat is named the *Ingeborg*," she told Ellen, "for Mama."

(Mama and Henrik are siblings)

3. A   "I meant to warn you. You must stay away from people while we are here."

"But there's no one around here," Annemarie reminded her.

"Even so. If you see anyone at all—even someone you know, one of Henrik's friends—it is better if you come in the house. It is too difficult—maybe even dangerous—to explain who Ellen is."

4. D   "Where is my necklace?" she asked. "What did you do with it?"

"I hid it in a safe place," Annemarie told her. "A very secret place where no one will ever find it. And I will keep it there for you until it is safe for you to wear it again."

5. B   Mama always teased him gently for not marrying; she asked him, laughing, when they were together, whether he had found a good wife yet, one who would keep his house tidier.

6. C   Do you know what I have done? I found enough apples for applesauce. Even though there is no sugar, the apples are sweet. Henrik will bring home some fish and there is wood for the fire, so tonight we will be warm and well fed."

"It is not a bad time, then," Annemarie told her.

"Not if there is applesauce."

7. D   Mama and Kirsti had gone inside, but Annemarie and Ellen ran across the high-grassed meadow, through the late wildflowers.

...

They tiptoed across the damp stones and let the water touch their feet. It was cold. They giggled and stepped back.

...

"Look," she said. "This leaf may have come from a tree in Sweden. It could have blown from a tree into the sea, and floated all the way across. See over there?" she said, pointing. "See the land? Way across there? That's Sweden."

8. There Has Been a Death

1. C   Although Uncle Henrik no longer raised crops on the farm, as his parents had, he still kept a cow, who munched happily on the meadow grass and gave a little milk each day in return.

2. B   "They do," she said. "They relocate all the farmers' butter, right into the stomach of their army! I suppose that if they knew Henrik had kept this tiny bit, they would come with guns and march it away, down the path!"

3. A   "And," she added, "there's butter, too. Usually not even Henrik has butter, but he managed to save a little this time."

"Save a little from what?" Annemarie asked, spooning oatmeal into a flowered bowl. "Don't tell me the soldiers try to —what's the word? —relocate butter, too?" She laughed at her own joke.

But it wasn't a joke at all, though Mama laughed ruefully. "They do," she said. "They relocate all the farmers' butter, right into the stomach of their army! I suppose that if they knew Henrik had kept this tiny bit, they would come with guns and march it away, down the path!"

Kirsti joined their laughter, as the three of them pictured a mound of frightened butter under military arrest.

...

Suddenly, here in this sunlit kitchen, with cream in a pitcher and a bird in the apple tree beside the door—and out in the Kattegat, where Uncle Henrik, surrounded by bright blue sky and water, pulled in his nets filled with shiny silver fish —suddenly the specter of guns and grim-faced soldiers seemed nothing more than a ghost story, a joke with which to frighten children in the dark.

4. B   Inside the house, Mama scrubbed and dusted, tsk-tsking at Uncle Henrik's untidy housekeeping. She took the rugs out to the clothesline and beat them with a stick, scattering dust into the air.

5. A   "Tomorrow will be a day for fishing," Henrik said, his smile disappearing.

Annemarie, listening, recognized the odd phrase. Papa had said something like it on the telephone. "Is the weather good for fishing, Henrik?" Papa had asked. But what did it mean? Henrik went fishing every day, rain or shine. Denmark's fishermen didn't wait for sunny days to take their boats out and throw their nets into the sea. Annemarie, silent, sitting with Ellen under the apple tree, watched her uncle.

6. C   Mama nodded. "It is cleaned, and I moved the furniture a bit to make room.

"And you saw the flowers," she added. "I hadn't thought of it, but the girls picked dried flowers from the meadow."

"Prepared the living room for what?" Annemarie asked. "Why did you move the furniture?"

...

"Well, girls," he said, "it is a sad event, but not too sad, really, because she was very, very old. There has been a death, and tonight your Great-aunt Birte will be resting in the living room, in her casket, before she is buried tomorrow. It is the old custom, you know, for the dead to rest at home, and their loved ones to be with them before burial."

7. A   Annemarie said nothing. She was confused. This was the first she had heard of a death in the family. No one had called Copenhagen to say that there had been a death. No one had seemed sad.

And—most puzzling of all—she had never heard the name before. Great-aunt Birte. Surely she would have known if she had a relative by that name. Kirsti might not; Kirsti was little and didn't pay attention to such things.

…

And Annemarie was quite, quite certain, though she said nothing. There was no Great-aunt Birte. She didn't exist.

9. Why Are You Lying?

1. D   "I think that is not true," Uncle Henrik said. "I think you are like your mama, and like your papa, and like me. Frightened, but determined, and if the time came to be brave, I am quite sure you would be very, very brave.

2. C   "But," he added, "it is much easier to be brave if you do not know everything. And so your mama does not know everything. Neither do I. We know only what we need to know.

3. B   "There is no Great-aunt Birte, and never has been. Your mama lied to you, and so did I.

"We did so," he explained, "to help you to be brave, because we love you. Will you forgive us for that?"

4. C   "You guessed correctly," he told her. "There is no Great-aunt Birte, and never has been. Your mama lied to you, and so did I.

"We did so," he explained, "to help you to be brave, because we love you. Will you forgive us for that?"

Annemarie nodded. She felt older, suddenly. "And I am not going to tell you any more, not now, for the same reason. Do you understand?"

5. D   "Friends of Great-aunt Birte," Mama said quietly in response to Annemarie's questioning look. Annemarie knew that Mama was lying again, and she could see that Mama understood that she knew.

…

Why hadn't these people brought food? Why didn't they talk? In Copenhagen, even though the talk was sad, people had spoken softly to one another and to Mama and Papa. They had talked about Lise, remembering happier times.

6. A   But she didn't. She understood that she was protecting Ellen the way her mother
had protected her. Although she didn't understand what was happening, or why
the casket was there —or who, in truth, was in it —she knew that it was better,
safer, for Ellen to believe in Great-aunt Birte. So she said nothing.

7. D   In a moment Uncle Henrik returned. Behind him was Peter Neilsen.

...

Ellen was still outside. But in a moment the door opened and she returned —held
tightly, like a little girl, her bare legs dangling, against her father's chest. Her
mother was beside them.

10. Let Us Open the Casket

1. A   The male, accented voice from the kitchen was loud. "We have observed," he
said, "that an unusual number of people have gathered at this house tonight.
What is the explanation?"

2. A   Annemarie watched as the man's eyes moved around the room. He looked for a
long time at the casket. Then he moved his gaze, focusing on each person in turn.
When his eyes reached her, she looked back at him steadily.
"Who died?" he asked harshly.
No one answered. They watched Annemarie, and she realized that the officer was
directing the question at her.

3. B   "I do know your customs," he said, turning his gaze toward Mama, who still
stood in the doorway. "And I know it is the custom to pay one's respects by looking your loved one in the face. It seems odd to me that you have closed this coffin
up so tightly." His hand was in a fist, and he rubbed it across the edge of the polished lid.

4. D   With a swift motion the Nazi officer slapped Mama across her face. She stag-
gered backward, and a white mark on her cheek darkened.

5. A   Mama walked quickly across the room, directly to the casket, directly to the officer. "You're right," she said. "The doctor said it should be closed, because Aunt
Birte died of typhus, and he said that there was a chance the germs would still be
there, would still be dangerous. But what does he know—only a country doctor,
and an old man at that? Surely typhus germs wouldn't linger in a dead person!"

6. D   Peter stood and drew the dark curtains across the windows. He relit the extin-
guished candle. Then he reached or the old Bible that had always been there, on
the mantel. He opened it quickly and said, "I will read a psalm."

His eyes turned to the page he had opened at random, and he began to read in a strong voice.

...

Mama sat down and listened. Gradually they each began to relax. Annemarie could see the old man across the room, moving his lips as Peter read; he knew the ancient psalm by heart.

7. D   Finally, still reading, he moved quietly to the window. He closed the Bible and listened to the quiet night. Then he looked around the room. "Now," he said, "it is time."

First he closed the windows. Then he went to the casket and opened the lid.

11. Will We See You Again Soon, Peter?

1. C   There was no one in the casket at all. Instead, it seemed to be stuffed with folded blankets and articles of clothing.

2. C   It was true that there had been few new clothes for anyone during the recent years; but still, Ellen's mother had always managed to make clothes for her daughter, often using old things that she was able to take apart and refashion in a way that made them seem brand-new. Never had Ellen worn anything so shabby and old.

3. B   "I'm sorry," he said to them. "There is nothing for a baby."
"I'll find something," Mama said quickly. "The baby must be warm." She left the room and was back in a moment with Kirsti's thick red sweater.

4. C   Peter's voice was firm. "We can't take a chance," he said. He inserted the dropper of the bottle into the baby's tiny mouth, and squeezed a few drops of liquid onto her tongue. The baby yawned, and swallowed. The mother closed her eyes; her husband gripped her shoulder.

5. A   Finally, Peter took a paper-wrapped packet from the inside of his own jacket.

...

"I want you to deliver this. Without fail. It is of great importance." There was a moment of silence in the hall, and Annemarie knew that Peter must be giving the packet to Mr. Rosen.

6. B   Annemarie's mother moved around the room and gave each person a small package of food: the cheese and bread and apples that Annemarie had helped her prepare in the kitchen hours before.

7. A   Annemarie realized, though she had not really been told, that Uncle Henrik was

going to take them, in his boat, across the sea to Sweden.

12. Where Was Mama?

1. B   "It's very dark," Mama whispered as they stood in the yard with their blankets and bundles of food gathered in their arms, "and we can't use any kind of light. I'll go first—I know the way very well—and you follow me. Try not to stumble over the tree roots in the path. Feel carefully with your feet. The path is uneven."
...
There were stars here and there, dotting the sky among thin clouds, but no moon.
...
It would be faster for Mama alone, with no need to wait as the Rosens, unfamiliar with the path, slowly felt their way along.

2. D   Then they were gone, Mama and the Rosens. Annemarie was alone. She went into the house, crying suddenly, and closed the door against the night.

3. C   She thought of Papa, back in Copenhagen alone. He would be awake, too. He would be wishing he could have come, but knowing, too, that he must come and go as always: to the corner store for the newspaper, to his office when morning came. Now he would be afraid for them, and watching the clock, waiting for word that the Rosens were safe, that Mama and the girls were here at the farm, starting a new day with the sun shining through the kitchen window and cream on their oatmeal.

4. B   The clock in the hall struck once; it was two-thirty in the morning. Her mother would be home in an hour, Annemarie decided.

5. D   Light woke her. But it was not really morning, not yet. It was only the first hint of a slightly lightening sky: a pale gleam at the edge of the meadow, a sign that far away somewhere, to the east where Sweden still slept, morning would be coming soon.

6. B   The door to the other bedroom, the one Kirsti and Mama were sharing, was closed. Quietly, not wanting to wake them, Annemarie pushed it open.
...
There was no one else in the wide bed.

7. B   After a second she saw a shape there: something unfamiliar, something that had not been there the day before. A dark shape, no more than a blurred heap, at the beginning of the path.

13. Run! As Fast As You Can!

1. C   "Can you believe it? I was very nearly here—well, maybe just halfway—when I tripped over a root and went sprawling."

2. A   Her mother pulled herself to a sitting position. She winced in pain. "I'm all right, really. Don't worry. And the Rosens are with Henrik. That's the important thing."

3. A   "You should have seen me, Annemarie," she said, shaking her head with a wry look. "Your proper mama, crawling inch by inch! I probably looked like a drunkard!"

4. B   "When we get inside, I'll have a cup of tea and then we'll call the doctor. I'll tell him that I fell on the stairs. You'll have to help me wash away the grass and twigs. Here, Annemarie, let me rest for a minute."

5. C   "Mama, what is this?" she asked suddenly, reaching into the grass at the foot of the steps.
Mama looked. She gasped. "Oh, my God," she said.
Annemarie picked it up. She recognized it now, knew what it was. It was the packet that Peter had given to Mr. Rosen.

6. A   "You must run to the boat. If anyone should stop you—"
"Who would stop me?"
"Annemarie, you understand how dangerous this is. If any soldiers see you, if they stop you, you must pretend to be nothing more than a little girl. A silly, empty-headed little girl, taking lunch to a fisherman, a foolish uncle who forgot his bread and cheese."

7. A   "Annemarie, you understand how dangerous this is. If any soldiers see you, if they stop you, you must pretend to be nothing more than a little girl."

14. On the Dark Path

1. A   She thought of a story she had often told to Kirsti as they cuddled in bed at night. "Once upon a time there was a little girl," she told herself silently, "who had a beautiful red cloak. Her mother had made it for her.
"She wore it so often that everyone called her Little Red Riding-Hood."

2. B   Annemarie smiled, feeling her way through the dark, remembering how Kirsti always interrupted stories to ask questions.

3. A   Here the path turned. She knew the turning well, though it seemed different in the dark. If she turned to the left, it would take her to the road, out where it would be lighter, wider, more traveled. But more dangerous, too. Someone could see her on the road.

4. D   Here the path widened and flattened; it was the place where the woods opened on one side and the path curved beside a meadow at the edge of the sea. Here she could run, and she did.

5. C   She had often come this way before, too, sometimes at the end of the afternoon, to pick out the Ingeborg, Uncle Henrik's boat, from the many returning, and to watch him and his helpers unload the day's catch of slippery, shimmering herring still flopping in their containers.

6. D   The bushes were overgrown and it was difficult to see the path here. But she found the entrance, beside the high blueberry bushes —how often she had stopped here, in late summer, to pick a handful of the sweet berries!

7. D   Then they were there, in front of her. Four armed soldiers. With them, straining at taut leashes, were two large dogs, their eyes glittering, their lips curled.

15. My Dogs Smell Meat!

1. B   Annemarie willed herself, with all her being, to behave as Kirsti would.

2. D   Annemarie nodded. "Yes," she said. One of the dogs growled. But she noticed that both dogs were looking at the lunch basket.

3. D   The soldier reached forward and grabbed the crisp loaf of bread from the basket. He examined it carefully. Then he broke it in half, pulling the two halves apart with his fists.

     ...

The soldier ignored her. He tossed the two halves of the loaf to the ground, one half in front of each dog. They consumed it, each snapping at the bread and gulping it so that it was gone in an instant.

4. A   "My dogs smell meat," the soldier said.

5. B   "What's that? There, in the bottom?" he asked in a different, tenser voice. What would Kirsti do? Annemarie stamped her foot. Suddenly, to her own surprise, she begin to cry. "I don't know!" she said, her voice choked. "My mother's going to be angry that you stopped me and made me late. And you've completely ruined Uncle Henrik's lunch, so now he'll be mad at me, too!"

     ...

The soldier took out the packet. "Why was this so carefully hidden?" he snapped.

6. A   He looked inside, then glared at Annemarie. "Stop crying, you idiot girl," he said harshly . "Your stupid mother has sent your uncle a handkerchief. In Germany the women have better things to do. They don't stay at home hemming handkerchiefs for their men."

7. A   "All is well," he said softly. "Don't worry. Everything is all right."

"I wasn't sure," he said. "But now"—he eyed the basket in his hands—because of you, Annemarie, everything is all right.

16. I Will Tell You Just a Little

1. C   But the noise from Blossom, forgotten, unmilked, uncomfortable, in the barn, had sent Annemarie warily out with the milking bucket. She had done her best, trying to ignore Blossom's irritated snorts and tossing head, remembering how Uncle Henrik's hands had worked with a firm, rhythmic, pulling motion. And she had milked.

2. B   "Many of the fishermen have built hidden places in their boats. I have, too. Down underneath. I have only to lift the boards in the right place, and there is room to hide a few people.

3. A   Peter, and others in the Resistance who work with him, bring them to me, and to the other fishermen as well. There are people who hide them and help them, along the way to Gilleleje."

4. D   Uncle Henrik nodded. "The dogs are trained to sniff about and find where people are hidden. It happened just yesterday on two boats. Those damn dogs, they go right through dead fish to the human scent.

5. B   "And they have created a special drug. I don't know what it is. But it was in the handkerchief. It attracts the dogs, but when they sniff at it, it ruins their sense of smell. Imagine that!"

6. C   "Did they bring dogs to your boat this morning?"

"Yes. Not twenty minutes after you had gone. I was about to pull away from the dock when the soldiers appeared and ordered me to halt. They came aboard, searched, found nothing. By then, of course, I had the handkerchief. If I had not, well—"

7. C   Uncle Henrik stood, and patted the cow's head. "I saw them ashore. There were people waiting to take them to shelter. They are quite safe there."

17. All This Long Time

1. B   For nearly two years, now, neighbors had tended the plants and dusted the furniture and polished the candlesticks for the Jews who had fled. Her mother had done so for the Rosens.

2. A   Peter had been captured and executed by the Germans in the public square at Ryvangen, in Copenhagen.

3. C   The Nazis refused to return the bodies of the young men they shot at Ryvangen. They simply buried them there where they were killed, and marked the graves only with numbers.

4. C   "She was part of the Resistance, too," Papa had explained. "Part of the group that fought for our country in whatever ways they could."

5. D   The whole day had been a blur of grief. "But what about Lise?" she asked. "If she wasn't shot, what happened?"

"From the military car, they saw her running, and simply ran her down."

6. A   She turned and went to her bedroom, where the blue trunk still stood in the corner, as it had all these years. Opening it, Annemarie saw that the yellow dress had begun to fade; it was discolored at the edges where it had lain so long in folds.

Carefully she spread open the skirt of the dress and found the place where Ellen's necklace lay hidden in the pocket. The little Star of David still gleamed gold.

7. A   "Can you fix this? I have kept it all this long time. It was Ellen's."

Her father took it from her and examined the broken clasp. "Yes," he said. "I can fix it. When the Rosens come home, you can give it back to Ellen."

"Until then," Annemarie told him, "I will wear it myself."

NUMBER THE STARS

1판 1쇄 2010년 12월 20일
2판 4쇄 2024년 9월 9일

지은이   Lois Lowry
기획 김승규
책임편집 김보경 유난영 이수영
콘텐츠제작및감수 롱테일 교육 연구소
저작권 명채린
마케팅 두잉글 사업 본부

펴낸이 이수영
펴낸곳 롱테일북스
출판등록 제2015-000191호
주소   04033 서울특별시 마포구 양화로 113, 3층(서교동, 순흥빌딩)
전자메일 help@ltinc.net

ISBN 979-11-91343-85-4 14740